ANTARCTIC JOURNEYS

First published in 2019 by New Holland Publishers
London • Sydney • Auckland

131-151 Great Titchfield Street, London WIW 5BB, United Kingdom
1/66 Gibbes Street, Chatswood, NSW 2067, Australia
5/39 Woodside Ave, Northcote, Auckland 0627, New Zealand

newhollandpublishers.com

A catalogue record for this book is available from the
National Library of New Zealand.

ISBN 9781869664992

Group Managing Director: Fiona Schultz
Publisher: Sarah Beresford
Project Editor: Rebecca Sutherland
Designer: Andrew Davies
Production Director: James Mills-Hicks
Printed in China by Easy Fame (Hong Kong) Limited

10 9 8 7 6 5 4 3 2 1

Keep up with New Holland Publishers on Facebook
facebook.com/NewHollandPublishers

Cover: Sunset at Port Charcot, Antarctica.
CREDIT PHILIPP SALVETER, SHUTTERSTOCK.
This spread: A mid-winter glow, Weddell Sea,
showing the Endurance, 1915. Taken by Frank
Hurley. CREDIT: MITCHELL LIBRARY, STATE LIBRARY
OF NEW SOUTH WALES [FILE NUMBER FL1114106]
Previous page: Our first guided walk out onto the
ice in front of Scott Base. CREDIT: PHILIPPA WERRY.

ANTARCTIC JOURNEYS

PHILIPPA WERRY

NEW
HOLLAND

Dedicated with thanks to Antarctica New Zealand, the Scott Base team of 2016–2017 and all those who have shared their knowledge, enthusiasm and passion for Antarctica with me. In the words of Apsley Cherry-Garrard, in his introduction to *The Worst Journey in the World*: 'Talk of ex-soldiers; give me ex-antarcticists, unsoured and with their ideals intact: they could sweep the world.'

ACKNOWLEDGEMENTS

Many people have generously given of their time and expertise to help me in writing this book. I would like to thank all of those who shared their knowledge of and passion for Antarctica and provided feedback on all or sections of the text.

In particular I would like to express my thanks and gratitude to the staff at Antarctica NZ (Megan Martin, Bailey Jeffery-Butler), NZ Antarctic Research Institute (Fiona Shanhun), Antarctic Heritage Trust (Lizzie Meek), NIWA (Craig Stevens, Natalie Robinson, Susan Pepperell), Deep South National Science Challenge (Alex Keebel), Dr David Harrowfield, and all of the Antarctica 2016/2017 team, especially Katrina Grenfell and Paul Lovegrove.

I would like to thank the many wonderful librarians, archivists and historians who have fielded my enquiries, including those at the Alexander Turnbull Library, National Library of New Zealand and Wellington Public Library.

Thanks also to Grace Blewitt (Air NZ), Tim Halpin (Airways Corp), Anthony Tedeschi (Alexander Turnbull Library), Jill Haley (Canterbury Museum), Aimee Kenworthy and Maria Adamski (Christchurch City Council), Phil Lyver (Manaaki Whenua Landcare Research), Thomas Adams (MetService), Jamie Mackay (Ministry for Culture and Heritage), Haritina Mogosanu (Museums Wellington), Luz Baguioro, Ross Hickey and Phil Murray (NZ Defence Force), Christopher Stephens (New Zealand Geographic Board Ngā Pou Taunaha o Aotearoa), Alan Hollows (NZ Post), Ann Martin (Te Awhina marae, Motueka), Nichola Vessey (Ngāti Rārua Ātiawa Iwi Trust), Carolyn McGill (Te Papa), Tug Lyttelton Preservation Society, Zel Lazarevich (Wellington Zoo); Inger Sheil (Australian National Maritime Museum), Suzanne Brassil and Tom Norquay (State Library of NSW), Helen Carter (Scott Polar Research Institute, Cambridge); Clare Beech and Øyvind Thuresson (Sandefjord Whaling Museum, Norway); John Long, Strategic Professor in Palaeontology, Flinders University, Adelaide, South Australia; Ted Daeschler, Curator of Vertebrate

Zoology, Academy of Natural Sciences, Professor, Department of Biodiversity, Earth and Environmental Science, Drexel University, Philadelphia, PA; Juliane Gross, Associate Professor, Dept. of Earth and Planetary Sciences, Rutgers University, NJ; Laura J. Kissel, Polar Curator, Byrd Polar and Climate Research Center, Ohio State University; Diane McKnight, Institute of Arctic and Alpine Research, Boulder, Colorado; Michael Lucibella, Editor, The Antarctic Sun, US Antarctic Program; Bill Spindler southpolestation.com; Jason Anthony; Terry Tickhill Terrell; Corey Baker, Anne Beresford and Sarah Fortescue, Agnieszka Fryckowska, Emily Fryer (Emily Fryer Conservation), Peter McCarthy, Bridget Mahy, Gabby O'Connor, Katja Riedel and Kim Westerskov.

New Holland Publishers have once again been a pleasure to work with and I am grateful for the care and attention they have given to this book. Thanks especially to my publisher Sarah Beresford, who has always been helpful, supportive and encouraging.

Special thanks to my daughter Charlotte for drawing the map of Antarctica and the diagram of the snow cave.

Lastly, huge thanks to my husband David who accompanied me on several expeditions to track down historic sites, monuments and memorials, and provided many of the images for this book.

TEXT ACKNOWLEDGEMENTS

Words of Margaret Mahy (p 6 and 97) reproduced by permission of Bridget Mahy from *The Riddle of the Frozen Phantom* (Collins, 2001).

Speech by Lianne Dalziel, 6 October 1917 (p 16) reproduced by permission of Mayor Lianne Dalziel.

'Heaven' from *The Ponies* (VUP, 2007) by Bernadette Hall; reproduced by permission of the author (p 23).

Words of Jason Anthony (p 63) reproduced by permission of the author from *Hoosh: Roast penguin, scurvy day and other stories of Antarctic cuisine* (University of Nebraska Press, c2012).

Words of John Long (p 63) reproduced by permission of the author from *Mountains of Madness* (Allen & Unwin, 2011).

Words of Juliane Gross (p 91) from her blog entries caslabs.case.edu/ansmet/category/17-18/ reproduced by permission of the author.

Titles, captions, inscriptions, newspaper reports and quotations are reproduced with the original punctuation and spelling. Units of measurement are quoted in miles if that was the standard at the time. 1 mile = 1.6km. (Note that the early explorers sometimes used geographic or nautical miles, which are slightly different from statute miles.)

"There is something wonderful about spinning out across Antarctic

snow and seeing mountains ahead of you, beautiful as dreams yet

somehow truer than dreams. Once you have seen those mountains

there is no waking up from them. They are in your head for always."

– Margaret Mahy, *The Riddle of the Frozen Phantom* (Collins, 2001)

CONTENTS

CREDIT: PHILIPPA WERRY.

Above: Sign at Scott Base showing distances to the South Pole and around the world
CREDIT: MARK JAMES, 2003–04, ANTARCTICA NEW ZEALAND PICTORIAL COLLECTION.

Introduction

Antarctica is like no other continent. People suspected it was there for centuries, but it was one of the last places in the world to be discovered. It has no **indigenous** inhabitants or language. Its early history is a saga of exploration and endurance in the face of raging storms, freezing temperatures, blizzards and ferocious winds, and it is told by and about men. No women stepped onto the continent for decades after the first sightings and landings.

Nobody lives there permanently. Everyone arrives from somewhere else and then leaves again. Antarctic animals carry out their own journeys and **migrations**. Even the ice moves across the landscape from the high mountains towards the sea.

This book tells the stories of Antarctic journeys, big and small, animal and human, scientific and practical, journeys of art and memory, journeys through the landscape and into the past.

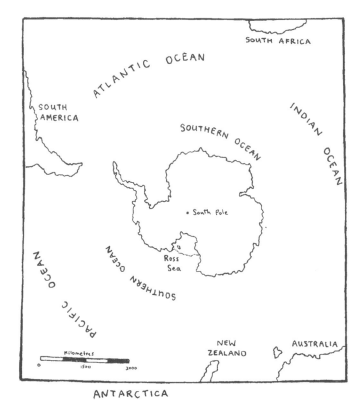

Above: Antarctica is bigger than Europe or the United States and nearly twice as big as Australia. It is often shown as a wiggly line at the bottom of the globe, but its actual shape is like a rough circle, with the Antarctic Peninsula sticking out towards South America. CREDIT: CHARLOTTE WERRY.

CHAPTER ONE

JOURNEYS OF EXPLORATION

THE FIRST ADVENTURERS

Today we have photographs, film footage and satellite images of Antarctica, but 300 years ago, there were no maps to show that it existed.

People from the South Pacific or South America may have known about it. Hui Te Rangiora, a Polynesian navigator who lived around 650 AD, appears in Rarotongan legend and in tribal stories of Ngāti Rārua and Te Āti Awa. He voyaged south in his waka Nga-Iwi-o-Aotea and found himself in a strange ocean full of huge white rocks which he called Te Tai Uka a Pia, or 'sea foaming like arrowroot' (a plant that grows in the Pacific). Another story tells how Tamarēreti sailed south with 70 chiefs and two tohunga on his waka Te Rua o Maahu to uncover the mystery of the white land and the blazing southern lights.

Centuries later, the first European explorers were awestruck with what they found: enormous icebergs, jigsaws of floating ice, **glaciers** spilling into the sea, cliffs of solid ice, chains of snow-covered mountains and even volcanoes. There were bays full of spouting whales, beaches crammed with seals and penguins, and albatrosses, petrels and skuas soaring overhead.

On 17 January 1773, Captain James Cook's ships *Adventure* and *Resolution* became the first recorded vessels to cross the **Antarctic Circle**. Cook never sighted the Antarctic coast, but he landed at South Georgia, one of the sub-Antarctic islands, in January 1775. It was cold, remote and bare. 'Not a tree or shrub was to be seen,' he wrote, 'no not even big enough to make a toothpick.'

Other explorers followed, including Fabian

Opposite: Mt Erebus (seen here from Castle Rock) is the world's southernmost historically active volcano, and taller than Aoraki Mt Cook.
CREDIT: PHILIPPA WERRY.

Right: The statue of Captain Cook in Victoria Square, Christchurch was sculpted by William Trethewey, who also created some remarkable World War One memorials.
CREDIT: DAVID WERRY.

von Bellingshausen, Nathaniel Palmer, James Weddell, Jules Dumont d'Urville, Charles Wilkes and James Clark Ross. Weddell gave his name to the Weddell Sea and also Weddell seals. In January 1841, Ross was the first person to get through the floating pack ice to the Ross Sea, named after him, as are Ross Island and the Ross Ice Shelf. (Mt Erebus and Mt Terror are named after his ships.) Tuati Peak in the Royal Society Range, Victoria Land, is named after the first recorded New Zealander to visit the Antarctic coast, a Māori man named Tuati (also known as John Sac) who sailed with Wilkes from 1838–40.

Sealers and whalers followed, too. When they heard about the huge numbers of wildlife, they headed south to start slaughtering seals, penguins and whales.

THE LAST UNCHARTED SPACE

Fridtjof Nansen, the great Norwegian explorer, pioneered new techniques for polar travel in the Arctic in his ship *Fram* (meaning 'Forward'). Meanwhile, Antarctica remained one of the last blank spaces on the globe. There was no way to get there except by sea, and the Southern Ocean was wild and dangerous to cross.

It took time, money, determination and hard work to choose a suitable team and organise a ship, food and stores for a year or more. Expedition leaders often helped to fund their trips by promising a scoop to a newspaper and by writing books and giving lectures afterwards. People were fascinated by polar exploration and flocked to hear or read about it.

THE HEROIC AGE

The 'heroic age' or 'heroic era' of Antarctic exploration was named for its mix of romance, heroism, adventure, daring and courage. It lasted for about 20 years, from 1895 until World War One, or perhaps until the death of one of the greatest explorers, Sir Ernest Shackleton, in 1922. The explorers were often described as heroic, but the term itself was coined later; Rev James Gordon Hayes wrote in *The Conquest of the South Pole* (1932) that 'as a small tribute to these gallant men it is suggested that this period should be known as the Heroic Era of Antarctic Exploration.'

During this time a series of expeditions headed south. Some are better known than others, some turned into almost unbelievable survival epics and some led to tragedy. They are

Below: Advertisement for an illustrated talk in Dunedin by Sir Ernest Shackleton. His audience in Christchurch, a few days earlier, 'hung on every word the explorer said, and was thrilled by his vivid story of the frightful odds which the men of the *Endurance* and the *Aurora* had to face in their grim fight with Death.' CREDIT: PRESS, 26 FEBRUARY 1917; OTAGO DAILY TIMES, 26 FEBRUARY 1917 (PAPERS PAST).

LECTURE.

KING'S THEATRE

TO-NIGHT!   TO-NIGHT!
At 8 o'clock.
Chairman, his Worship the Mayor.

SIR ERNEST SHACKLETON
Will Deliver an
ILLUSTRATED LECTURE
On
ANTARCTICA
Relating the
DANGERS,
ADVENTURES,
And
THRILLING EXPERIENCES
Met with by his Gallant Band from
Day to Day.
ILLUSTRATED with Beautiful Lantern
Views Taken by Members of the
Expedition.

Proceeds in Aid of the Dependents of
Captain M'Intosh (who lost his life at the
South Pole) and the Red Cross Society.
Box Plan at The Bristol; Day Sales at
S. Jacobs's. Dress Circle and Orchestral
Stalls, 4s; Stalls, 3s; Pit, 2s.
At the Piano, Mr J. A. Haggitt.

WITH
CAPTAIN SCOTT, R.N. TO THE SOUTH POLE
(BRITISH ANTARCTIC EXPEDITION)
FILMED BY HERBERT G. PONTING, F.R.G.S.

AWAITING OUR ARRIVAL.

AUTHENTIC PICTURES EXHIBITED BY ARRANGEMENT WITH
THE GAUMONT Cº Lᵀᴰ LONDON
HOLDERS OF EXCLUSIVE CINEMATOGRAPH RIGHTS

Above: Herbert Ponting, the photographer on the *Terra Nova*, filmed the Polar Party setting off but returned to England in 1912, so the first audiences watching this film didn't yet know what had happened to Scott and his companions. CREDIT: REF: EPH-E-ANTARCTICA-1912-02. ALEXANDER TURNBULL LIBRARY, WELLINGTON, NEW ZEALAND.

usually identified by date, title and the name of the leader, the ship and the hut used as a **base**.

Men joined these expeditions from many countries: America, Argentina, Australia, Britain, Belgium, Canada, Chile, France, Germany, Japan, New Zealand, Norway, Sweden and Uruguay. They were sailors, scientists, Navy officers, dog-handlers, cooks, artists, doctors, photographers and enthusiastic amateurs. Together they mapped land and coastlines, carried out scientific studies and measurements, recorded weather conditions and collected fossils, rocks, animal skins and penguin eggs. They formed strong friendships and some of them died together.

BELGIAN ANTARCTIC EXPEDITION
DATES: **1897–99.** LEADER: **Adrien de Gerlache.** SHIP: *Belgica*

The *Belgica* sailed from Antwerp, Belgium, on 16 August 1897, heading for South America and then Antarctica. On board as First Mate was a young Norwegian called Roald Amundsen. The ship's doctor, Frederick Cook, was American. As the *Belgica* threaded its way through icy waters studded with icebergs, Cook wrote 'we are as hopelessly isolated as if we were on the surface of Mars.'

Adrien de Gerlache took his ship so far south (intentionally or not) that it became trapped in the ice. 'We are part of an endless frozen sea,' wrote Cook, 'the first of all human beings to pass through the long antarctic night.' Nobody knew what this would be like. At first, the crew went out onto the ice to toboggan, ski and hunt animals for food. They sang and whistled, played the accordion, danced and told funny stories. But as the dark set in, many of them became 'sad and dejected, lost in dreams of melancholy ... tired of everything.' Cook saved them with his 'baking treatment': an hour in front of a hot fire, cheerful attention and plenty of fresh meat to ward off **scurvy**.

Everyone was elated when the sun returned after 71 days of total darkness. The *Belgica* broke free of the ice at last and returned to Punta Arenas, Chile, in March 1899. Cook described how the sailors 'kicked about in the sand and tossed pebbles ... with the delight of children at the seashore.' The officers set off up the road to find a hotel, but after being at sea for so long, they found it hard to walk straight. 'We spread our legs, dragged our feet, braced and balanced our bodies with every step, and altogether our gait was ridiculous.' A woman – the first they had seen for months – stared at the rough-looking men in their patched clothes, gathered up her children and rushed inside.

Below: Crevasses in the ice pose a constant danger. Some are easily visible, like this one; others are covered by a snow bridge and not as obvious (Australasian Antarctic Expedition, 1911–1914).
CREDIT: MITCHELL LIBRARY, STATE LIBRARY OF NEW SOUTH WALES [FILE NUMBER FL917736].

BRITISH ANTARCTIC EXPEDITION
DATES: 1898–1900.   LEADER: **Carsten Borchgrevink.** SHIP: *Southern Cross*

Carsten Borchgrevink led the first planned winter-over. The ten men, including five Norwegians and two Lapps who looked after the dogs, built two wooden huts at Cape Adare. Over winter, they collected scientific data, slept a lot and got sick of eating the same food day after day. There were high points: amazing **aurora**, a dog that was swept out to sea on an ice floe but reappeared a week later, celebrations for the anniversary of Norway's separation from Denmark and Queen Victoria's birthday. But they felt homesick and became grumpy and quarrelsome. 'The sameness of those cold dark nights attacks the minds of men like a sneaking evil spirit,' wrote Borchgrevink.

The saddest part of their expedition was when the zoologist Nicolai Hanson fell ill. He had been eager to see the Adélie penguins return to their breeding grounds in spring, and he was shown the first one just before he died on 14 October 1899. Hanson never saw his baby daughter, Johanne, who was born after he left home. The men wrapped him in a Norwegian flag, with dried flowers and ferns from Norway and Tasmania, and buried him at a spot he had chosen. The ground was frozen like iron and they had to dynamite it to dig a hole.

Borchgrevink said they were longing 'to see something else but bare rocks and snow, to see other colours, real green grass and, above all, *trees*.' Returning home via New Zealand, they sailed into Paterson Inlet on Stewart Island on 31 March 1900. After being isolated for so long, they found it strange to meet new people and to catch up with world news. One of the first questions they were asked was whether they had found any people living 'down there'.

THE RACE TO THE SOUTH POLE
The first explorers had reached Antarctica, but it was still a long way to the South Pole. There was no known route, and compasses wouldn't help because they point to the South **Magnetic Pole**, not the Geographic Pole. The ice was crisscrossed with mazes of deep chasms and **crevasses**, temperatures were below freezing and **frostbite**, snow blindness and scurvy were serious risks.

The distances were huge. From Scott Base to the South Pole is about the same distance as Sydney to Adelaide, or Seattle to San Francisco. The 2700km return trip is almost as far as the Te Araroa trail, which runs the length of New Zealand for 3000km, and all this had to be covered on foot.

There was no shelter, no firewood and no-one to help if anything went

Left: Statue of Captain Scott on the corner of Worcester Street and Oxford Terrace, Christchurch. CREDIT: DAVID WERRY.

The statue of Captain Scott in Christchurch was designed by his widow Kathleen, a sculptor, and unveiled in front of a big crowd on 9 February 1917. Kathleen Scott created several statues of her husband. This one was going to be made in bronze, but metal was needed for the war effort, so she used white Italian marble – and never quite finished the gloves. The statue was badly damaged when it toppled over in the February 2011 earthquake. It was carefully repaired and put back in position in October 2017. Captain Scott still faces north as if on his homeward journey, but now he stands on base isolators against any further quakes.

"A century ago, this statue honoured our Antarctic history, today it honours that and much more. May it inspire our children to become our modern day explorers – our researchers and scientists – who will help secure the future of our world."
(Lianne Dalziel, Mayor of Christchurch, speech at unveiling 6 October 2017)

wrong. Crossing the mountains at high altitudes made the men dehydrated, but there was no water except by melting snow. Every bit of gear, tents, food and fuel had to be hauled by dogs, ponies, machines or men, with supply parties making extra trips to lay **depots** in advance. Even practical tools like the Primus portable stove were new. Without the Primus, invented in Sweden in 1892, it would have been impossible to cook hot food and melt snow into water on a long trek over the ice.

It would be a terribly hard journey, but a huge achievement for whoever got there first. Soon the newspapers were calling it a 'Race for the Pole'.

Three famous contenders in the 'Race' were Robert Falcon Scott, Ernest Shackleton and Roald Amundsen. Two of these men were British and one was Norwegian. Two got to the South Pole, and one never did, despite three attempts. They had very different personalities, leadership styles and planning methods. All three of them were to die in polar regions.

BRITISH NATIONAL ANTARCTIC EXPEDITION
DATES: **1901–04.** LEADER: **Robert Falcon Scott.** SHIP: *Discovery.*
BASE: **Hut Point**

Scott's first expedition was partly organised by the Royal Geographical Society and the Royal Society. Scott was a Navy officer who expected to have the last say over any decisions. The hut, modelled on an Australian bungalow, was too cold to live in, so they ate and slept on board the *Discovery*, which remained iced in over the winter. The *Discovery* men collected scientific data, found fossils, mapped previously unknown land including the Dry Valleys, charted the coastline and discovered the emperor penguin colony at Cape Crozier. Scott, Edward Wilson and Shackleton, who was also on this expedition, went further south than anyone before in their attempt to reach the South Pole. They ran short of food on the return journey, but Scott felt that Shackleton, who suffered the worst from scurvy, was holding them back. When a support ship arrived in early 1903, bringing extra supplies, Scott ordered Shackleton to leave on medical grounds.

Right: The Christchurch statue needed painstaking conservation work to restore it after the February 2011 earthquake. Other memorials to Scott are in Warkworth, Port Chalmers and Queenstown. CREDIT: EMILY FRYER CONSERVATION; CHRISTCHURCH CITY COUNCIL.

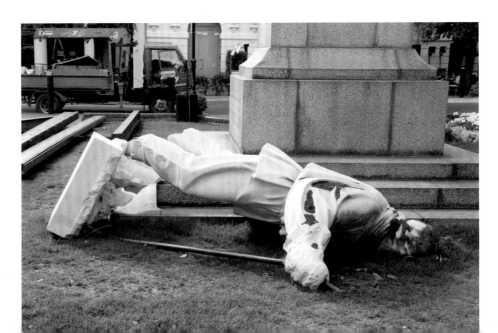

BRITISH ANTARCTIC EXPEDITION

DATES: **1907–09.** LEADER: **Ernest Shackleton.** SHIP: *Nimrod.*
BASE: **Cape Royds**

Shackleton managed to scrabble together the funds for his own expedition. Like Scott, he used New Zealand as his last base and a large crowd farewelled the *Nimrod* from Lyttelton on 1 January 1908.

Shackleton brought the first ponies and the first car to Antarctica. The *Nimrod* men were the first to climb Mt Erebus and the first to (almost) reach

Left: Crowd at Lyttelton Wharf, Christchurch, to witness the departure of the *Nimrod* for Antarctica (1908). CREDIT: REF: 1/2-040918-G. ALEXANDER TURNBULL LIBRARY, WELLINGTON, NEW ZEALAND.

Below: The tug *Lyttelton*, now over 110 years old, escorted the *Nimrod* out to sea when it left for Antarctica on 1 January 1908. Today it is lovingly cared for by the Tug Lyttelton Preservation Society. CREDIT: DAVID WERRY.

the South Magnetic Pole. Shackleton made the decision, followed by later expeditions, to send his ship back to New Zealand for the winter, instead of keeping it trapped in the ice. In spring, he set off with Eric Marshall, Jameson Adams and Frank Wild for the South Pole.

'It is a wonderful place we are in,' he wrote on 25 November 1908. 'There is an impression of limitless solitude about it all that makes us feel so small as we trudge along, a few dark specks on the snowy plain.' Christmas Day found them 'lying in a little tent, isolated high on the roof of the end of the world.' The high altitude caused headaches and nose bleeds and the wind knocked them off their feet. They got to within 100 miles of the South Pole, but Shackleton chose to stop at that point. He always put his men first and didn't think they would survive the return journey if they kept going. 'Whatever regrets may be,' he wrote on 9 January 1909, 'we have done our best.'

On the way back, they were 'appallingly hungry'. As they walked, they planned elaborate future meals out loud, and at night they dreamed about food. At times, they only had one day's ration left until they found the next depot. 'Our food lies ahead,' Shackleton wrote on 21 February, 'and death stalks us from behind.' But they got back safely, without suffering from scurvy, and after travelling further south than anyone before.

Watch silent footage of Shackleton's British Antarctic Expedition, Departure from Lyttelton, New Zealand, 1908 on YouTube (Archives New Zealand).

NORWEGIAN ANTARCTIC EXPEDITION
DATES: 1910–12. LEADER: **Roald Amundsen**. SHIP: *Fram*.
BASE: **Framheim**

Roald Amundsen first went to the Antarctic on the *Belgica*. Later, in the Arctic, he made friends with the Netsilik people (Canadian Inuits) who taught him about cold weather clothing, igloo building and travelling on ski with sledges and dogs. His dream was to reach the North Pole, but when he heard that two other people had done so, he decided to try for the South Pole instead. Worried about losing funding, he kept this a secret until his ship *Fram*

Right: In Hobart, Amundsen kept the result of his expedition secret until he knew that his chosen newspaper had received the story first, so other papers could only guess and wait. CREDIT: AUCKLAND STAR, 8 MARCH 1912, PAPERS PAST.

RACE FOR SOUTH POLE.

———

DID SCOTT WIN IT?

———

AMUNDSEN BACK FROM ANTARCTIC.

———

A MYSTERIOUS MESSAGE.

———

EXPLORER WILL REVEAL NOTHING.

(once used by Nansen) reached Madeira, where the routes north and south diverged. There he gave his men the chance to leave (but none did) and sent a telegram to Scott: *Beg leave to inform you Fram proceeding Antarctic. Amundsen.*

Fram arrived in the Bay of Whales on 14 January 1911 with 116 dogs on board. Amundsen built his hut, Framheim, on the ice barrier, not on land (like Scott's huts on Ross Island). This meant he was slightly closer to the Pole than Scott, but it was also a gamble because there was a chance that the ice would break off, taking the hut with it. His luck held and that didn't happen.

Amundsen used his Arctic experience to plan everything meticulously. His team spent the winter mending clothing, improving equipment and repacking provisions to save space. They made the sledges lighter and sewed a tent cover to keep their tent warm and dark. After an early start, when it was too cold and they had to return, Amundsen set off again on 20 October with four sledges, about 50 dogs and four other men: Helmer Hanssen, Sverre Hassel, Olav Bjaaland and Oscar Wisting. They were all good skiers – Bjaaland was a Norwegian ski champion – they had warm reindeer fur clothing and they were used to handling dogs. They came across crevasses that were big enough to swallow the *Fram*, but they made good progress and often covered 20–30km a day.

On 14 December 1911, they planted the Norwegian flag together at the South Pole. For three days, they explored and measured around the area to make sure they were at the exact spot. They left a tent with spare equipment, clothing and a letter for the King of Norway, asking Scott to send it for them. This would prove that they had arrived first if anything happened to them on the return trip. They marked all their equipment with the words 'South Pole' and the date, to be used as souvenirs, and went into the tent one by one to write their names on a tablet fixed to the tent pole.

On the way back they easily found all their depots, marked by black flags on a line of bamboo poles. They had so much food that they fed their extra biscuits to the dogs. After 99 days, they reached Framheim two weeks ahead of schedule, and left for Australia a few days later. On 7 March 1912, Amundsen came ashore in Hobart, Tasmania, and booked into Hadley's Orient Hotel while he cabled the story of his success. Once the news broke, reporters came flocking and the crew of the *Fram* were feted and celebrated.

Amundsen spent the rest of his life exploring the northern polar regions. He disappeared in the Arctic in June 1928, flying to search for survivors of an airship crash. His plane also probably crashed and those on board were never found.

Opposite: Newspaper headlines show the worldwide shock felt when the fate of Scott and his men became known. CREDIT: STAR (11 FEBRUARY 1913), TIMARU HERALD AND SOUTHLAND TIMES (12 FEBRUARY 1913) PAPERS PAST.

BRITISH ANTARCTIC EXPEDITION
DATES: **1910–13.** LEADER: **Robert Falcon Scott.** SHIP: *Terra Nova.*
BASE: **Cape Evans**

Scott waded through thousands of applications from men keen to join his second expedition. The *Terra Nova* left from Cardiff, Wales on 15 June 1910. In Melbourne, Scott was taken aback to receive Amundsen's telegram saying he was also heading south. They took on extra supplies at Lyttelton and left New Zealand from Port Chalmers on 29 November. The *Terra Nova* was heavily laden and sailed almost straightaway into such a fierce storm that they feared the ship might sink. On 4 January 1911, they chose a headland (called Cape Evans) on Ross Island for their base and started to unload the ship and build their prefabricated hut.

Before winter, they sent off parties to explore and to lay supply depots. They had skiing lessons from Tryggve Gran, the one Norwegian team member, and played hockey and football. Then they settled in for the long, cold months of darkness. They kept busy feeding and exercising the dogs, caring for the ponies, listening to gramophone records, reading, painting, celebrating midwinter and birthdays, writing letters and diaries, producing a newspaper, developing photos, giving lectures and slideshows, playing chess, dominoes and backgammon, taking weather and scientific observations and repairing equipment.

Scott insisted that scientific discoveries were as important as reaching the Pole – but the Pole was a tantalising goal. He sent his first men off on 24 October 1911 with the motor sledges (which soon broke down), followed by others with ponies and dogs. They followed Shackleton's route up the Beardmore Glacier,

FIVE EXPLORERS PERISH.

Captain Scott and Companions Dead.

Overtaken by Blizzard.

They Had Reached South Pole.

Terra Nova's Early Return.

Due To Disaster.

(Extraordinary Press Association Message.)
(Received February 11, 8.10 a.m.)
LONDON, February 10.
A remarkable and painful sensation has been caused throughout the city by the receipt of a cablegram from New Zealand conveying news of a dreadful disaster to Captain Scott's South Polar Expedition.
The leader of the expedition himself and his four companions on the Polar journey are dead.
They had reached the South Pole on January 18, 1912. On the return journey they were overtaken by a blizzard and perished.

THE GRIM ANTARCTIC

Its First Great Tragedy.

DEATH OF CAPTAIN SCOTT AND FOUR COMRADES.

THE GOAL ATTAINED.

Story of Heroism and Endurance.

SCOTT'S PATHETIC FAREWELL.

(Per Press Association.—Copyright.)

Yesterday morning a Press Association message was received from London conveying the startling information that Captain Scott and his party of four, who made the final dash for the Pole, perished in a blizzard, after reaching the Pole, on January 18.
The news caused a painful world-wide sensation.

POLE PARTY LOST !

CAPTAIN SCOTT AND FOUR COMPANIONS

AFTER REACHING POLE

DIE ON RETURN JOURNEY.

FROM SICKNESS AND BLIZZARD.

Received 8.10 a.m., February 10th.
LONDON, Feb. 10.
EXTRAORDINARY.—News that Captain Scott and party perished in a blizzard, after reaching the Pole on January 18th, has caused a sensation.

with some men turning back at each stage until Scott chose his companions for the last push: Edward Wilson, Henry Bowers, Lawrence Oates and Edgar Evans. These five reached the South Pole on 17 January 1912. The day before, they glimpsed a flicker of a black flag in the distance and saw dog prints in the snow. They knew then that Amundsen had beaten them.

Bitterly disappointed, they started the trek back. Evans had a fall, later collapsed and died on 17 February. 'Amongst ourselves we are unendingly cheerful, but what each man feels in his heart I can only guess,' Scott wrote on 3 March. A few days later he added wistfully, 'We still talk of what we will do together at home.'

Above: Amundsen used dogs to pull his sledges, but Scott still believed in the value of 'manhauling', which was much harder work than it appears here. Taken by Herbert Ponting, October 1911. CREDIT: AUSTRALIAN NATIONAL MARITIME MUSEUM [ANMM COLLECTION 00053066] / FLICKR COMMONS.

Left: Sleeping quarters inside Cape Evans hut. This section, nicknamed 'the Tenements', was home to Cherry-Garrard, Bowers, Oates, Meares and Atkinson. Taken by Herbert Ponting, October 1911. CREDIT: AUSTRALIAN NATIONAL MARITIME MUSEUM [ANMM COLLECTION 00053958] / FLICKR COMMONS.

Oates, crippled with frostbite, limped out of the tent into a blizzard on or about 16 March to give his companions a chance of continuing without him. His last words, according to Scott, were: 'I am just going outside and may be some time.' Scott, Wilson and Bowers were trapped by bad weather only 11 miles from a food depot. Too ill to move, they spent their last days writing farewell letters and diary entries.

We shall stick it out to the end, but we are getting weaker of course and the
end cannot be far. It seems a pity, but I do not think I can write more.
R. Scott.
For God's sake, look after our people.
(Scott's final diary entry, 27 March 1912)

The men back at the Cape Evans hut waited and waited for Scott and his team to return. On 19 April, Tryggve Gran recorded in his diary how he heard a loud banging at the door and rushed to open it, hoping against hope that the five men might have survived. Outside stood a large emperor penguin.

HEAVEN

A galaxy of stars on dark water,
the breaking of the pack.

Or more like fat congealing on boiled mutton.

When there is white only,
when everything is coloured white,
the land, the sky, the ice and the horizon,

the heroes as they walk away
you'd say were climbing a white wall to heaven.

by Bernadette Hall in *The Ponies* (VUP, 2007)

Opposite: The dejected Polar Party at the South Pole, 18 January 1912. They know by now that Amundsen has beaten them. Ponting, the photographer, had shown Bowers how to use a long thread to release the shutter and take the photograph, so they could all be included. CREDIT: AUSTRALIAN NATIONAL MARITIME MUSEUM [ANMM COLLECTION 00053983] / FLICKR COMMONS.

Later that year, in spring, a search party found the bodies, diaries and letters inside the tent. The sledge held rock samples which Scott and his men had hauled all the way from the Beardmore Glacier. There was no sign of Oates' body, only his reindeer-skin sleeping bag (now in the Scott Polar Research Institute in Cambridge, England) and one boot. The search party held a short burial service and covered the tent with a **cairn** of snow and a cross made of skis. The skis were Gran's and he used Scott's skis to return to Cape Evans, saying that at least they would complete the journey.

Back in New Zealand, the *Terra Nova* crept into the harbour at Oamaru at 2.30am on the morning of 10 February 1913, 'like a phantom ship', as Cherry-Garrard described it. Harry Pennell and Edward Atkinson went ashore to cable a report before catching the train to Christchurch, but the ship had to stay at sea until the news had been officially released, to make sure the story didn't leak out. By the time Atkinson and Pennell rejoined the *Terra Nova* at Lyttelton, the news had broken. Flags flew at half mast, church bells tolled and newspaper headlines blared the first shocked reports. 'It's made a tremendous impression,' Atkinson said to Cherry-Garrard. 'I had no idea it would make so much.'

For a long time, Scott was viewed as the tragic hero of a tale of endurance and courage. Later he was criticised as a risk taker and bad planner. Some people blamed his last-minute decision to take five men, not four, to the Pole, when the rations were planned for four. Other historians have studied weather reports and concluded that he was a victim of unusually bad weather for that time of year.

JAPANESE SOUTH POLAR EXPEDITION
DATES: **1910–12.**   LEADER: **Nobu Shirase.** SHIP: *Kainan Maru*

On 8 February 1911, the people of Wellington were surprised to see a small wooden ship entering the harbour. This was the *Kainan Maru* ('Southern Pioneer'). For centuries, Japanese people had not been allowed to travel abroad. Very few Japanese had ever been to New Zealand and the crew spoke little English. When Lieutenant Nobu Shirase and some of his men came ashore, a fascinated crowd trailed after them to the Post Office, where they bought stamps for letters home, and to a restaurant for dinner.

The *Kainan Maru* headed south, but they had left too late in the season and the sea ice barred their way. They decided to sail to Sydney for the winter and try again later in the year. In Sydney, where they camped at Parsley Bay, some people suspected they were spies, but Professor Edgeworth David (who had been on the *Nimrod*) stood up for them. When they left in November 1911, they presented Professor David with a 17th century samurai sword, now in the Australian Museum in Sydney, as a gesture of thanks and friendship.

Above: Plaque on the Wellington waterfront in memory of the *Kainan Maru's* visit in 1911. CREDIT: DAVID WERRY.

In Antarctica, the *Kainan Maru* came across the *Fram* in the Bay of Whales, but the language barrier prevented much communication. Shirase led a small team on a 'dash patrol' and planted the Japanese flag on their furthest point south. They returned to a great welcome in Yokohama, but the excitement soon died away and Shirase was left owing a lot of money. He sold the *Kainan Maru* and died in 1946, poor and almost forgotten, but today his name is on a museum in his home town, a Japanese **ice breaker** and on the Shirase coast in the Ross Sea. Nobu Shirase, who dreamed of being a polar explorer as a child, led the first non-European Antarctic expedition, explored an unknown part of the continent and got all his men safely home.

Journeys of endurance

Scott's Northern Party

Six *Terra Nova* men formed the Northern Party: Victor Campbell (nicknamed 'the wicked mate'), Dr George Levick, Raymond Priestley and three Navy seamen, Harry Dickason, Frank Browning and George Abbott. They planned to explore east of Cape Evans, but *Fram* was already there. Instead, on 18 February 1911, the *Terra Nova* dropped them on the beach at Cape Adare. This was where Borchgrevink and his men had stayed.

Campbell's team built their own hut and spent ten months exploring and wintering over. On 4 January 1912, the *Terra Nova* returned and took them further south. For six weeks, they sledged, explored, camped in tents, climbed mountains and crossed glaciers. Then they waited for the ship, but it couldn't reach them through the ice. Eventually they realised they would have to winter over again, this time with little food, no hut and tents that were falling to pieces.

The men dug a snow cave to be their home. It was entered by crawling down a passage and the floor was covered with pebbles, gravel and dried seaweed. Six sleeping bags and the stove took up nearly all the room inside. The class system was still strong in the Navy, so they drew an imaginary line down the middle, between officers and sailors, and each pretended they couldn't hear what was said on the other side.

They killed seals and penguins for food, sometimes finding a surprise meal of undigested fish, and learned to eat fried **blubber** as well as meat. Birthdays were marked with an extra biscuit, a stick of chocolate or six raisins as a treat. They held concerts, with all the songs they could remember, and did exercises to keep

Right: Plan of Northern Party cave, based on the drawing in Raymond Priestley's *Antarctic Adventure*. There was barely room to move inside the cave, or even to stand upright.
CREDIT: CHARLOTTE WERRY.

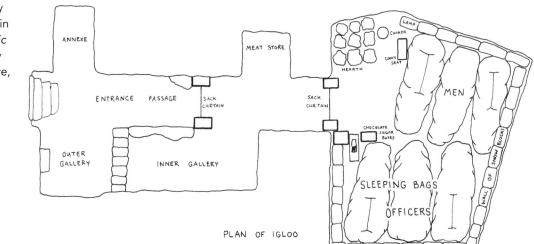

fit. At night they read out loud a chapter or two from the books they had with them and talked about their plans for the future.

The men shared cooking duties in teams of two; when not on duty, they spent hours dozing in their sleeping bags (like 'huge and hairy caterpillars', Priestley said). The lamps, made from melted oil and string, filled the cave with 'smitch' (oily brown smoke from burning blubber) and the snow roof melted all over their bags. Cooking in near darkness led to some nasty results.

> It was impossible to see plainly either in the cave or in the passage outside, and so the ice which was melted for the tea and cocoa-water was frequently dirty with blubber, while lumps of seaweed from the floor also often found their way into the tea … There are few sensations so unpleasant as swallowing a mass of slimy seaweed when one is not prepared for it.
> (Raymond E. Priestley, *Antarctic adventure*)

In October, as daylight returned, they began the 230-mile trek across the sea ice back to Cape Evans, hauling their gear on sledges. They had no idea what had happened to Scott's men, and nobody at Cape Evans knew if they were still alive or not. Their story has been overshadowed by the fate of the Polar Party, but it was an amazing tale of endurance and courage.

Fifty years later, in 1963, a New Zealand field party found the entrance to the snow cave, still with its seal skin roof and bamboo marker flag. In 2016, a 100-year old fruit cake, probably left behind by the Northern Party, was found during conservation work on Borchgrevink's hut.

THE WORST JOURNEY IN THE WORLD

Apsley Cherry-Garrard (nicknamed Cherry), one of the youngest on the *Terra Nova* expedition, wrote a book afterwards titled *The Worst Journey in the World*. He didn't mean Scott's trek to the Pole, but his midwinter journey with Henry 'Birdie' Bowers and Edward 'Uncle Bill' Wilson to an emperor penguin rookery at Cape Crozier, 65 miles from Cape Evans. Wilson wanted to collect emperor penguin eggs, and they had to go in winter because that was when the birds nested.

The three men set off on 27 June 1911, pulling a heavy sledge in darkness. Cherry said it was so cold that ice formed in their beards and they could hear their breath crackle as it froze in mid-air. Each night, the men had to try and thaw a way into their sleeping bags, which had become solid slabs.

Right: Wilson, Bowers and Cherry-Garrard back at the Cape Evans hut after their 'worst journey'. Taken by Herbert Ponting. CREDIT: AUSTRALIAN NATIONAL MARITIME MUSEUM [ANMM COLLECTION 00053963] / FLICKR COMMONS.

At Cape Crozier they built a rock hut to sleep in and stored their gear in the tent. They climbed down dangerously icy cliff faces to reach the penguins, then scrambled up again in the dark, clutching five precious eggs, Cherry stumbling the most because he was so short-sighted. The weather was already terrible, but it got even worse. Back at their campsite a howling blizzard sprung up, whipped the canvas lid off their stone hut and blew their tent away.

'The earth was torn in pieces,' Cherry wrote, 'the indescribable fury and roar of it all cannot be imagined.' For two days, the men hunkered down in their sleeping bags with nothing to eat except handfuls of snow and a few sweets. They sang songs and hymns, and every so often they kicked each other to make sure they were still alive. Without a tent, they knew they wouldn't survive the return trip, and there was little chance of finding it again.

The storm died down. They started to look for the tent anyway, and then a miracle occurred.

> I followed Bill down the slope. We could find nothing. But, as we searched, we heard a shout somewhere below and to the right. We got on a slope, slipped, and went sliding down quite unable to stop ourselves, and came upon Birdie with the tent, the outer lining still on the bamboos. Our lives had been taken away and given back to us.
>
> We were so thankful we said nothing.
>
> (Apsley Cherry-Garrard, *The Worst Journey in the World*)

After 35 days, with their clothes frozen like sheets of armour to their bodies, they arrived back at the safety of Cape Evans. 'Antarctic exploration is seldom as bad as you imagine, seldom as bad as it sounds,' Cherry wrote. 'But this journey had beggared our language; no words could express its horror.' It was so bad that his teeth split and shattered in the cold.

Only one of the three would return home. Bowers and Wilson died on the way back from the South Pole, but Cherry never forgot his friends and how they had stayed kind, polite and generous through such a terrible ordeal. 'They were gold, pure, shining, unalloyed,' he wrote. 'Words cannot express how good their companionship was.'

Of the five emperor penguin eggs they collected, Cherry broke two by accident. (He wondered if the oil left in his gloves helped to save his fingers from frostbite.) Back in London, he took the precious eggs to the Natural History Museum. At the time, the museum staff didn't seem very interested, but today the eggs are among the museum's most treasured objects.

In 1957, Sir Edmund Hillary and a group of New Zealanders retraced the trip with tractors and found the remains of the stone walls of the hut by reading the description in Cherry's book. They collected some relics including thermometers, a pick-axe and a sledge, now held by museums in New Zealand.

Below: Australasian Antarctic Expedition members inside the hut at Cape Denison, 1911–1914. CREDIT: MITCHELL LIBRARY, STATE LIBRARY OF NEW SOUTH WALES [FILE NUMBER FL1005462].

Above: Blizzard at Cape Denison, 1912. Frank Hurley was trying to capture the force of the wind in this image of men struggling to perform their outdoor duties. He built a shelter from blocks of ice to photograph them from, but his fingers still got frostbitten and at one stage he was lifted up by a gust of wind, along with his heavy camera and tripod, and flung several metres away onto the rocks. CREDIT: MITCHELL LIBRARY, STATE LIBRARY OF NEW SOUTH WALES [FILE NUMBER FL917731].

AUSTRALASIAN ANTARCTIC EXPEDITION

DATES: **1911–14** LEADER: **Douglas Mawson.** SHIP: *Aurora.* BASE: **Cape Denison**

Douglas Mawson, the most famous Australian Antarctic explorer, travelled with Shackleton on the *Nimrod* and was part of a three-man, 1260-mile journey to locate the South Magnetic Pole. In 1911, he led his own expedition and set up base at Cape Denison, not realising that it was one of the windiest places in the world (his book about it was called *Home of the Blizzard*). He was interested in science, not in reaching the Pole, and his men made important discoveries over a huge area of the continent south of Australia.

In November 1912, Mawson, Belgrave Ninnis and Xavier Mertz set off with dogs, sledges and food for nine weeks, planning to be back before the *Aurora* came to collect everyone in mid-January. On 14 December, Mertz was skiing ahead, with Mawson in the middle, followed by Ninnis. The first two crossed a crevasse which seemed safe, but Mawson called a warning to Ninnis anyway. He heard nothing except 'a faint, plaintive whine from one of the dogs.' Then he looked back.

Behind me nothing met the eye except my own sledge tracks running back in the distance. Where were Ninnis and his sledge? I hastened back along the trail … The lid of the crevasse that had caused me so little thought had broken in; two sledge tracks led up to it on the far side – only one continued beyond.

(Douglas Mawson, *Home of the Blizzard*)

Ninnis had vanished suddenly and completely. After calling out for hours, they held a burial service for him and turned back. Dogs, one sledge, their tent and extra clothing had been lost and they had so little food that they had to kill and eat the remaining dogs. Mertz became too weak to walk and he died in their makeshift tent on 8 January 1913.

Now Mawson was completely alone. He was so sick that his hair started to fall out and a complete layer of skin came off the soles of his feet, but he bandaged them up, put on more socks and kept going. Once he fell into a crevasse but managed to haul himself up on the rope. On 8 February, he reached the hut at Cape Denison. Hours earlier, the *Aurora* had sailed away to collect the other party stationed further west, leaving six men behind as a search team. They all faced a second Antarctic winter before the *Aurora* came back for them.

Mawson led BANZARE (the British-Australian-New Zealand Antarctic Research Expedition) in 1929–31 and his picture featured on the Australian $100 note. Sir Edmund Hillary reckoned that his solo journey was one of the greatest of all survival stories.

Above left: Dog teams scouting a way to the land across the rough sea ice; Shackleton expedition; taken by Frank Hurley. CREDIT: MITCHELL LIBRARY, STATE LIBRARY OF NEW SOUTH WALES [FILE NUMBER FL1114129].

Above right: Frank Hurley photographing under the bows of the *Endurance*, 1915. When the ship went down, he had to throw out most of his camera gear and choose which photos to save. CREDIT: MITCHELL LIBRARY, STATE LIBRARY OF NEW SOUTH WALES [FILE NUMBER FL1114099].

IMPERIAL TRANS-ANTARCTIC EXPEDITION

DATES: 1914–17   LEADER: **Ernest Shackleton**. SHIP: *Endurance*.
BASES: **Ocean Camp, Patience Camp, Elephant Island and South Georgia**

In 1914, Shackleton set out to cross the Antarctic continent from the Weddell Sea to the Ross Sea, but he never even reached his starting point because the *Endurance* became trapped in the ice. The men lived on board as long as possible, and before the ship was crushed and finally sank, they offloaded as much gear and food as they could, as well as the three lifeboats. For five months, they lived on ice floes that they named Ocean Camp and Patience Camp. Cracks in the ice were a constant danger. Once a floe cracked open right under one of the tents. Shackleton scooped Ernest Holness in his sleeping bag out of the sea, just before the two halves of the floe snapped together again.

They also worried about orca, which they called 'killers' (for killer whales).

'All around we could hear the killers blowing, their short, sharp hisses sounding like sudden escapes of steam … They would throw aside in a nonchalant fashion pieces of ice much bigger than our boats when they rose to the surface, and we had an uneasy feeling that the white bottoms of the boats would look like ice from below.

(Ernest Shackleton, *South*)

The ice floes gradually drifted towards the open water and then they scrambled into the lifeboats and rowed and sailed for a week to Elephant Island. All three boats made it, but they were still far from rescue. Shackleton chose five men to come with him on the largest lifeboat, the *James Caird*, named after a wealthy Scotsman who had helped fund the trip. On 24 April 1916, they set off. 'We stood on the beach,' Frank Hurley remembered, 'watching the tiny sail grow smaller and smaller until it diminished to a minute speck. How lonely it looked. Then it disappeared from sight.'

The six-man crew sailed 800 miles across the wild, wintry Southern Ocean to South Georgia. This was a triumph of navigation by Frank Worsley, who used the sun to fix position, despite only seeing it four times in 17 days. If he had made a mistake, they would have been swept on to oblivion. Every day they came close to being capsized, including once by the biggest wave Shackleton had ever seen. 'We peered under the clew of the sail and said encouragingly to each other, "She'll do it," even when we felt it most impossible,' Frank Worsley wrote. 'For nine hours we fought at its height a hurricane so fierce that, as we heard later, a 500-ton steamer from Buenos Ayres to South Georgia had foundered in it with all hands, while we, by the grace of God, had pulled through in a twenty-two-foot boat.'

They landed safely, but on the opposite side of the island from the Norwegian whaling settlement of Stromness. Shackleton, Worsley and Tom Crean set off to find a route across the inner mountain range with its peaks, cliffs, glaciers and gaping crevasses. They travelled 40 miles in 36 hours, sometimes by moonlight, with barely any rest. Shackleton once let the others go to sleep but didn't dare do so himself in case none of them ever woke up. He roused them after five minutes, telling them they'd slept for half an hour.

Below left: The *Endurance* frozen in the Weddell Sea and the dogs with their 'dogloos'. CREDIT: MITCHELL LIBRARY, STATE LIBRARY OF NEW SOUTH WALES [FILE NUMBER FL3181751, NO 40].

Below right: The men of the *Endurance* on either Ocean or Patience Camp. CREDIT: MITCHELL LIBRARY, STATE LIBRARY OF NEW SOUTH WALES [FILE NUMBER FL3181822, NO 164].

The first people they saw at Stromness were two young boys, who ran away, alarmed by the men's ragged beards, matted hair and torn, dirty clothing. The community had heard no word of the expedition for months and the manager at the whaling station, who knew Shackleton, at first didn't realise it was him, and was astonished to hear his story.

A ship was sent to fetch Timothy McCarthy, John Vincent and Harry McNeish, who had stayed with the *James Caird* (they didn't recognise Worsley, now clean and shaven) but it took Shackleton four months and four attempts in four different boats before he could reach the 22 men left behind on Elephant Island, with Frank Wild as their leader. They had lived inside a hut made by turning the two other lifeboats over, and everyone had survived, although they had to carry out an operation to amputate Perce Blackborow's frostbitten toes.

When Hurley spotted the rescue ship, he called to the others who were having lunch.

They came crawling through the roof, and breaking through the walls, frantic with joy … It was not only the sight of relief that warmed our hearts, for as the little boat drew near, we recognised our long-lost and heroic comrades, Shackleton, Crean and Worsley!
(Frank Hurley, *Argonauts of the South*)

Below left: The men left behind on Elephant Island wave goodbye to the *James Caird* as it sets off on its perilous journey. CREDIT: MITCHELL LIBRARY, STATE LIBRARY OF NEW SOUTH WALES [FILE NUMBER FL3181759, NO 48].

Below right: The Chilean tug *Yelcho* arrives with Shackleton on board, to save the men marooned on Elephant Island. Taken by Frank Hurley. 1916. CREDIT: MITCHELL LIBRARY, STATE LIBRARY OF NEW SOUTH WALES [FILE NUMBER FL3181767, NO 56].

THE ROSS SEA PARTY

DATES: **1914–17** LEADER: **Aeneas Mackintosh.** SHIP: *Aurora.*
BASE: **Cape Evans**

Shackleton had another team, the Ross Sea Party, under Aeneas Mackintosh. Their job was to set out a line of depots that Shackleton could use on the second half of his planned expedition, once he had passed the South Pole.

Mackintosh and his men left Hobart in the *Aurora* and used the Cape Evans hut as their base. *Aurora* was meant to stay through the winter, but was hurled out to sea in a storm in May 1915 and couldn't get back through the ice. (Two anchors, wrenched off at the time, remain buried near the hut.) The ship took with it most of the clothing, food, fuel and gear for the ten men left onshore, as well as the supplies for Shackleton, but the Ross Sea Party was determined to carry out their task. They hunted through the jumbled stores and boxes in the hut and killed seals to add to the food supply for them and the dogs. Over winter, they sewed pairs of trousers out of an old canvas tent and visited Shackleton's hut at Cape Royds to look for anything useful.

When spring arrived, they performed a series of terrible journeys in blizzards and freezing temperatures, hauling huge quantities of supplies to create the depots. They were haunted by the fear that Shackleton and his men would perish for lack of food, and it would be their fault. They drove themselves to the edge of exhaustion and starvation. What they didn't know was that Shackleton and his men weren't even coming. They were trapped on the ice on the *Endurance.*

Some of the men were suffering badly from scurvy. Arnold Spencer-Smith, the chaplain and photographer, became increasingly weak and died on 9 March

Left: One of the anchors of the *Aurora,* left behind when the ship was forced out to sea in a storm. CREDIT: PHILIPPA WERRY.

1916. The other men holed up at the *Discovery* hut until the sea ice was strong enough to cross to Cape Evans, but Mackintosh and Victor Hayward insisted on trying to get there and were lost in a blizzard. Nothing was found of them but their last footsteps, stopping abruptly in the ice.

Meanwhile the *Aurora* spent months trapped in the ice before she could struggle free. Short of coal, she limped into harbour at Port Chalmers, Dunedin, on 2 April 1916. The Ross Sea Party faced another long, gruelling Antarctic winter before Shackleton and the *Aurora* could come back for them. They arrived in Wellington on 9 February 1917, just a few hours after the unveiling of Captain Scott's statue in Christchurch.

JOURNEYS INTO BATTLE

In August 1914, war was declared. Thousands of young men marched off to fight and many lost their lives on the hills of Gallipoli, the fields of Flanders and France and the desert sands of the Middle East. Herbert Ponting was Scott's photographer on the *Terra Nova* and his films were shown to over 100,000 officers and men of the British Army. An army chaplain wrote to him: 'The splendid story of Captain Scott is just the thing to cheer and encourage out here.'

After the *Endurance* set off at the very beginning of the war, Shackleton and his men were cut off from any news, but they often talked about what might be happening. Nearly two years later, after crossing South Georgia, Shackleton asked the manager at the whaling station, 'Tell me, when was the war over?' and was staggered by his reply.

'The war is not over,' he answered. 'Millions are being killed. Europe is mad.

Right: Cemetery at Gallipoli. Bob Bage, from Mawson's *Aurora* expedition, is buried at Beach Cemetery, Anzac Cove. Nearby in the same cemetery is the grave of another Anzac hero, John Simpson Kirkpatrick or 'the donkey man'. CREDIT: PHILIPPA WERRY.

'The world is mad.' (Shackleton, *South*)

The men from *Terra Nova*, *Aurora* and *Endurance* returned from the isolation of the south to a world caught up in war. Many signed up as soon as they could. (Norway was neutral in World War One but Tryggve Gran signed up with the Royal Flying Corps.) Some died during the war, and others died later from the lingering effects of poison gas and other injuries. William Knowles from the *Terra Nova* was shot in an ambush in southern Turkey on 8 February 1915. One of the first New Zealanders to be killed as a result of enemy action, he died on board ship later that night and was buried at sea.

Edward (Bob) Bage was astronomer, assistant magnetician and recorder of tides on Mawson's *Aurora* expedition. He was cheerful, hardworking and liked by everyone. Back home, he got engaged, then enlisted and went off to Egypt with the Australian Engineers. He landed at Gallipoli on 25 April 1915. Less than two weeks later, he was killed near Lone Pine after being ordered to go out in broad daylight to lay marker pegs.

Shackleton dedicated his book *South* 'To my comrades who fell in the white warfare of the south and on the red fields of France and Flanders.' One of those comrades was Timothy McCarthy, who helped sail the *James Caird* to South Georgia. He went down with his ship when it was torpedoed by a German U-boat off the Irish coast in March 1917. Timothy's brother Mortimer was on the crew of the *Terra Nova*. Years later, in 1963, he was invited back to Antarctica with two other *Terra Nova* veterans; aged 80, he was the oldest person to have been there.

Frank Hurley, photographer, led a life of adventure after running away from home at 13 to find a job. He persuaded Mawson to take him on the *Aurora* by buying a ticket on the same train and talking to him for hours. Hurley sailed on the *Endurance* and later became Australia's official war photographer. His first night in London coincided with a German air raid and he pondered how strange it was that 'this madness was the civilisation we had been yearning to return to.' Later, on the Western Front, he wrote in his diary that the Menin road 'is the most gruesome shambles I have ever seen, with the exception of the Sth Georgia Whaling Stations, but here it is terrible as the dead things are men & horses.' [17 September 1917]

Left: Timothy and Mortimer McCarthy were one of two sets of brothers to sail with Scott and Shackleton. This monument to them overlooks the sea in their home town of Kinsale, Ireland.
CREDIT: PHILIPPA WERRY.

ADMIRAL BYRD AND LITTLE AMERICA

After the war, Admiral Richard Evelyn Byrd led five American expeditions to Antarctica, starting in 1928 and ending with Operation Deep Freeze in 1955–57. His base was called Little America. On his second trip, he set up the Bolling Advance Weather Base, about 120 miles south of Little America, to collect weather data from inland. He decided to staff this hut all by himself over the winter of 1934.

Living on his own, and in darkness, things could go wrong very quickly. He once got lost when he went for a walk and lost sight of his trail of bamboo markers. He saved himself by heaping up a pile of snow, walking out from there in different directions while counting his steps, and returning to the snow pile if he couldn't spot the last bamboo stick. Eventually he found it, 129 steps away.

Another time he went out into a blizzard to fix one of the weather instruments. He could hardly see or even breathe in the whirling snow and had to crawl on

Below left and right: The Byrd memorial sits on top of Mt Victoria, Wellington, shaped like a triangular polar tent. Inside, the bronze bust of Admiral Byrd is surrounded by rocks from Antarctica. The coloured ceramic tiles, by artist Doreen Blumhardt, depict the Aurora Australis or southern lights, and the compass points show that the memorial is pointing south. CREDIT: DAVID WERRY.

hands and knees in the wind. Back at the hut, he pulled at the trapdoor handle, but it was stuck tight and wouldn't budge. Fighting down panic, and rapidly getting colder, he lay down and kicked around with his feet until he found a shovel, then used the handle as a lever and got the trapdoor open. He had been outside for less than an hour but he was so exhausted that he went straight to bed, realising that he had nearly died with only a trapdoor between him and safety. Eventually, in July, he had to be rescued because he got sick from carbon monoxide poisoning caused by a faulty stove.

On his first trip, in November 1929, Byrd and three others flew from Little America to the South Pole and back in just over 18 hours, although they may not have flown over the exact spot. Some years later, in December 1935, Lincoln Ellsworth and Herbert Hollick-Kenyon completed the first trans-Antarctic flight, from Dundee Island on the Antarctic Peninsula to Little America. They were held up by bad weather so it took them nearly three weeks, including walking for days at the end after running out of fuel. Their plane, the *Polar Star*, is on display at the National Air and Space Museum, Washington, D.C.

ED HILLARY AND HIS TRACTOR EXPEDITION

Decades after the *Endurance* was lost in the ice, the Commonwealth Trans-Antarctic Expedition (TAE) aimed to complete the trip that Shackleton never finished. Dr Vivian 'Bunny' Fuchs would lead a party from the Weddell Sea to the South Pole and on to the Ross Sea, which he estimated would take 100 days. This was during the International Geophysical Year, or **IGY** (1957–58).

Sir Edmund Hillary, famous for climbing Mt Everest with Sherpa Tenzing Norgay in 1953, was chosen as leader of the Ross Sea team. Their job was to build Scott Base (the New Zealand scientific centre) at McMurdo Sound, mark out a route and lay a series of depots, meet Fuchs and his men at the last depot and guide them back. (Antarctic expeditions were still male-only at this stage.)

Fuchs' team was late setting off and blizzards, crevasses and vehicle problems slowed them down. Meanwhile, Hillary and his team headed steadily south on three converted Massey-Ferguson tractors, painted red to make them stand out, pulling sledges laden with cargo for the depots. They also had a caboose (like a caravan on skis) for cooking and sleeping in. On 15 December 1957, they reached the meeting point at Depot 700 (700 miles from Scott Base), but Fuchs hadn't yet got to the South Pole.

Hillary thought it made no sense to wait, using up valuable food and fuel. Poor radio contact made communications tricky and he didn't have formal

Opposite: Edmund Hillary being welcomed by Americans on completion of crossing. CREDIT: PHOTOGRAPHER UNKNOWN, 1957–59, ANTARCTICA NEW ZEALAND PICTORIAL COLLECTION.

Above: Sir Edmund Hillary introducing a husky pup to children at Dunedin in 1956. Some schools raised money to help buy dogs for Hillary's expedition to Antarctica. CREDIT: GEOFFREY LEE MARTIN, 1956–58, ANTARCTICA NEW ZEALAND PICTORIAL COLLECTION.

Above: Sir Edmund Hillary on a Massey Ferguson tractor leaving Depot 480 in December 1957 on his way to the South Pole. CREDIT: GEOFFREY LEE MARTIN, 1956–58, ANTARCTICA NEW ZEALAND PICTORIAL COLLECTION.

permission to keep going, but he did anyway. The tractors rumbled on and Ed Hillary, Murray Ellis, Jim Bates, Derek Wright and Peter Mulgrew reached the South Pole on 4 January 1958, with one barrel of fuel to spare. Nobody had reached the Pole by vehicle before; in fact, no groups had arrived overland since those of Scott and Amundsen. They were flown out, leaving the tractors behind, and Hillary flew back to meet Fuchs on 20 January 1958. The TAE reached Scott Base on 2 March, after 3473km and 99 days crossing the continent.

Unusual journeys

On 4 February 1902, Scott went up in a balloon, hoping to see further over the ice. Mawson meant to bring the first airplane, but it was damaged on a display flight in Australia. He took it anyway as an 'air tractor', or motorised sledge-pulling device, but it wasn't a success. Shackleton brought the first car: an Arrol-Johnston two-door open-top motor car. It had been adapted to run in cold conditions, but in heavy snow the wheels got stuck and the petrol engine didn't work well. A spare wheel was left at the hut but nobody knows what happened to the car itself.

Scott brought three 'motor sledges' on the *Terra Nova*, hoping they would replace horses or dogs. The biggest one fell through the ice and sank when being offloaded from the ship. The other two broke down early on their first journey and had to be left behind.

Below left: Ivan the Terra Bus is often the first Antarctic vehicle that people come across, because it is used for transport between the airfield and McMurdo Station or Scott Base. CREDIT: PHILIPPA WERRY.

Today, people use small aircraft, helicopters, tractors, Hagglunds and skidoos to get around, but some people still travel on foot and look for records to break. Henry Worsley (related to Frank Worsley from the *Endurance*) aimed to retrace Shackleton's intended route across the continent on foot. An ex-army officer, he was raising money for a charity for wounded soldiers and he broadcast daily updates heard around the world. After 71 days, he had to call for help on his satellite phone, 30 miles from his planned finish. He was airlifted out but died on 24 January 2016 in Punta Arenas. His family buried his ashes near Shackleton's grave in South Georgia.

Here are some more journeys for you to find out about:

- The Swedish South Polar Expedition of 1901–1904, led by Nils Otto Gustav Nordenskjöld (what happened to them and how were they rescued?)
- Erich von Dryalski and the crew of the *Gauss* in 1902 (what did they use ash and soot for?)
- The *Quest* expedition of 1921–22 (who died on board and where was he buried?)
- David Lewis, who sailed out of Sydney harbour in the *Ice Bird* on 19 October 1972 to circumnavigate the Antarctic continent (did he succeed?)
- Norwegian explorers Erling Kagge, Liv Arnesen and Børge Ousland (what records did they set?)

Below: The Hagglund is an all-terrain amphibious vehicle; its wide tracks and lightweight body help it to operate over snow and sea ice. CREDIT: PHILIPPA WERRY.

Below right: Børge Ousland coming to the end of his journey – an unassisted solo crossing of Antarctica. CREDIT: PHOTOGRAPHER UNKNOWN, 1996–97, ANTARCTICA NEW ZEALAND PICTORIAL COLLECTION.

THE FIRST WOMEN TO ANTARCTICA

For many years, Antarctica was a male-only continent, where heroes battled the elements and made exciting new discoveries, and there seemed no place for women in that picture.

Places like Adélie Land, Dronning Maud Land, Marguerite Bay and Victoria Land were named after explorers' wives or daughters or royalty. Apart from

that, women were only present in their photographs and letters. Wives and mothers like Kathleen Scott, Emily Bowers, Emily Shackleton and Gladys Mackintosh waited and hoped at home, with no news for months or years. Some women never saw their loved ones again. Kathleen Scott learned of her husband's death while sailing from California to New Zealand to meet him. Oriana, wife of Edward Wilson, was already waiting in New Zealand and heard the news from newspaper headlines.

THREE SPORTY GIRLS

When Shackleton announced his Imperial Trans-Antarctic Expedition, he received thousands of applications. Among them was a letter dated 11 January 1914 from Peggy Pegrine, Valerie Davey and Betty Webster, who called themselves 'three sporty girls' and declared they were 'willing to undergo any hardships'.

> We have been reading all books and articles that have been written on dangerous expeditions by brave men to the Polar-regions, and we do not see why men should have all the glory, and women none, especially when there are women just as brave and capable as there are men.

Shackleton wrote a few days later to thank them, but they didn't get a place on his ship.

The first women to get close to Antarctica were the wives of whalers. Ingrid Christensen sailed on four whaling trips in the 1930s. On her first trip, she and her friend Mathilde Wegger became the first women to see Antarctica. In March

Left: Ingrid Christensen (left) and Mathilde Wegger on a voyage in 1931. CREDIT: SANDEFJORD WHALING MUSEUM, NORWAY.

Opposite top: Dr Lois Jones, the leader of the all-women scientific expedition to the Dry Valleys, to the left of her green polar tent. Lake Vanda is in the background with its permanent ice cover. CREDIT: BILL SPINDLER (SOUTHPOLESTATION.COM) AND RADM WELCH, US NAVY (RET).

Opposite bottom: Dr. Jones and her three team members, taking a sample from the glacier ice melt Vanda River, which flows into Lake Vanda. CREDIT: BILL SPINDLER (SOUTHPOLESTATION.COM) AND RADM WELCH, US NAVY (RET).

1931, Douglas Mawson on the BANZARE expedition spotted two women on the deck of a Norwegian whaling ship – much to his astonishment – and it was probably these two women whom he saw. Caroline Mikkelsen, whose husband was the captain of another whaling ship, went ashore with a landing party in 1935 to raise the Norwegian flag, and for a long time was said to have been the first woman to step onto the continent. It is now thought that they landed on an island, and the honour of being the first woman on the mainland may fall to Ingrid, who landed at Scullin Monolith on 30 January 1937.

In 1947, Finn Ronne led the Ronne Antarctic Research Expedition to winter over on the Peninsula and asked his wife Jackie to come along. Jennie Darlington – newly married to Harry Darlington, the chief pilot – was also invited as her female companion. The idea of women in Antarctica was so unusual that it made the *New York Times* (24 March 1947) but they were still seen as less important than the men. The newspaper described them as 'attractive' and didn't give their names (only the names and roles of their husbands). Jennie had never cooked or sewed before, but she made red curtains out of an old horse blanket for her and Harry's small room at the end of the bunkhouse, and baked her first-ever cake for the midwinter dinner. Aged only 22, she also ended up helping the men with their long-distance relationship problems.

Women travelled on the first tourist boats, but being a visitor was different from working as a scientist. Female scientists heard the same excuses over and over: the harsh environment would be too tough for them; there were no bathroom facilities, no separate accommodation and no suitable women's

Above: Eileen McSaveney (left) and Terry Tickhill use a hand augur to drill Lake Vanda, Wright Valley, during their 1969–1970 field season. They were collecting water that was used to date the lake. CREDIT: TERRY TERRELL (FORMERLY TERRY LEE TICKHILL).

Above left: The historic moment when women first arrived at the South Pole. News media had been asking who would be the very first woman to step off the plane, so they decided to do it together. The six of them walked down the ramp arm-in-arm with Rear Admiral David F. 'Kelly' Welch, then the Commander, Naval Antarctic Support Force.

Above right: At the Geographic South Pole: Pamela Young, Jean Pearson (science reporter), Terry Lee Tickhill, Lois Jones, Eileen McSaveney and Kay Lindsay (Dry Valleys team). CREDIT BOTH: BILL SPINDLER (SOUTHPOLESTATION. COM) AND RADM WELCH, US NAVY (RET).

clothing. Professor Maria Klenova, a Russian marine geologist, was the first woman to do research in the Antarctic in 1956, but when Admiral Reedy called Antarctica 'the womanless white continent of peace' in 1965, many men were used to it being that way. The idea of women in Antarctica was treated as a joke; newspapers asked if they knew where it was or how they would cope without shops or hairdressers.

FOUR WOMEN IN THE DRY VALLEYS

In 1969–70, a four-woman science team from Ohio State University carried out field work in the Dry Valleys. The National Science Foundation was ready to send women before that, but the US Navy refused to take them. Finally they agreed, with conditions: it would be an all-woman team, so there was no need to share living spaces with men; they would work 200 miles from McMurdo Station and if there were any problems, no women would ever be allowed to come back – so they knew they couldn't make any mistakes.

Terry Lee Tickhill was a 19-year-old chemistry student when she was offered a place on the team as cook and field assistant. The women lived in a small hut and in tents in the Dry Valleys. They kept in touch with home by writing letters and giving them to the helicopter pilots who came to check on them every so often. Sometimes they went back to McMurdo Station for a few days and could telephone home, but the calls went through ham radio operators who passed on the speaker's words, so there was no chance of a private conversation.

Terry had never been more than 100 miles from her home in Ohio before.

She loved the fieldwork and being in such a beautiful wild place, and her time there, including surviving a helicopter accident, shaped the rest of her life. 'When I got to the ice I felt like a kid on a holiday,' she says. 'The whole Antarctic experience changed my outlook on life to that of an adult.' These four women paved the way for others to follow, and today about one third of American scientists in Antarctica are female.

First to McMurdo, Mawson and the South Pole

Patricia Hepinstall and Ruth Kelly, American air hostesses, flew on the first commercial flight from Christchurch to McMurdo Sound on 15 October 1957. During their 3½ hour visit, they judged a beard growing competition (categories included longest, bushiest, curliest and most unusual), took part in a dog sled race and were named Queen Bees of the Sea Bees (from CB, or Construction Battalion of the US Navy). On their way back to the United States, there was such interest in their story that they had to be flown home early for TV and radio interviews.

The first Australian woman to visit Antarctica was artist Nel Law, who went with her scientist husband Philip to Mawson Station in 1960–1961. She helped form the Antarctic Wives' Association to support women whose husbands worked far away in a place that most of them could never visit. Marie Darby, a New Zealand zoologist, went to Scott Base as a guest lecturer on the *Magga Dan* in January 1968. Dorothy Braxton, a journalist, had tried many times to overcome the 'petticoat ban' keeping women out before she managed to get a place on the second tourist cruise of the *Magga Dan*.

Pamela Young was the first New Zealand woman to live and work in Antarctica. She spent the summer of 1969–70 at the Cape Bird penguin rookery with a field party led by her husband. A clothing factory donated two pairs of women's woollen long johns, so she wouldn't have to wear men's ones. Pamela Young was also one of the first six women to reach the South Pole. The six (including the Dry Valleys team and a science reporter) were flown to the Pole on a US Navy plane on 12 November 1969. They were only there on a day visit; no women stayed overnight at the South Pole until 1971 and no women wintered over there until 1979.

Today many women live and work in Antarctica as scientists, expedition leaders, station managers, conservators, tour guides, technicians, support staff, mechanics, pilots, drivers, writers and artists.

CHAPTER TWO

TODAY'S JOURNEYS

CONSERVATION AND THE HUTS

Antarctica is the only continent where the first structures built by humans are still standing, and they have always been special places. Sir Edmund Hillary told a reporter that he once saw Shackleton's ghost walking forward to welcome him inside the Cape Royds hut.

Huts built by one expedition were used by later ones for shelter or to raid goods left behind. Some of the *Terra Nova* men, going to visit Cape Royds, found a batch of bread on the table, with teeth marks visible on the bread rolls. Outside, there were still hoof marks visible in the snow. Raymond Priestley, who had lived there on Shackleton's *Nimrod* expedition, felt as if his old companions might walk back in at any moment. The men took away with them some tins of jam, a plum pudding and gingerbread, and feasted on them that night.

The huts on Ross Island and McMurdo Sound were deserted for many years, but with the IGY and the founding of the American base at McMurdo Station and Scott Base, there was renewed interest in them. By now they had filled up with ice and snow and the furniture was encased in solid frozen blocks. Teams of workers spent several summers at Cape Evans and Cape Royds, working

Below left: Three men shovel snow from Shackleton's Hut, Cape Royds.
Below right: Ted Gawn clearing out the doorway of Shackleton's Hut.
CREDIT BOTH: PHOTOGRAPHER UNKNOWN, 1957–58, ANTARCTICA NEW ZEALAND PICTORIAL COLLECTION.

Left: In December 1960, the US Navy brought Sir Charles Wright, aged 73, back to Antarctica for the 50th anniversary of the *Terra Nova* expedition. Here he is visiting Shackleton's hut at Cape Royds and chuckling over a greasy frying pan found on the old stove. At Cape Evans, he stood beside the bunk that used to be his and helped the restoration team to work out the hut layout. CREDIT: PHOTOGRAPHER UNKNOWN, 1960–61, ANTARCTICA NEW ZEALAND PICTORIAL COLLECTION.

with picks and shovels to clear out cubic metres of snow, ice and rubbish. They carried blocks of ice outside to thaw in the sun so that the frozen contents could be retrieved.

Among the items they found were old boots and gloves, handmade clothing, candles, boxes of matches that still worked, sleeping bags, sledges, pony snowshoes and harnesses, a bicycle, magazines, books and letters, the chemicals in Ponting's darkroom, penguin eggs and a preserved emperor penguin that Wilson had been working on. There was lots of food, often still edible: cartons of biscuits, bottles of sauces and pickles, golden syrup, custard powder and sardines.

Caretakers looked after these two huts and acted as guides for visitors each summer from 1969 through the 1970s. One caretaker wrote that they sometimes felt like intruders, expecting 'the door to open at any moment and the sledging parties to return,' and that it would hardly have been a surprise to find 'a fur-clad

Top and above: Cape Evans hut, exterior and interior, showing the 'Tenements' bunks on the right. CREDIT: PHILIPPA WERRY.

figure sitting at the table, or moving about the stables.' (*Antarctic* v 6 no 2 June 1971) The huts were cared for by the Historic Sites Management Committee from 1980 until the New Zealand Antarctic Heritage Trust (AHT) was formed in 1993 to care for the bases in the Ross Sea area. The AHT has conserved the huts at Hut Point, Cape Evans and Cape Royds, Hillary's hut at Scott Base, and many thousands of artefacts, and is working on Borchgrevink's hut at Cape Adare.

THE JOURNEY OF A BISCUIT

Many early visitors quietly took away a souvenir or two, and relics ended up in museums and private collections all around the world. Nobody knows how many souvenirs were pocketed before the Antarctic Treaty and the Antarctic Heritage Trust gave the huts and their contents more protection. But at least one souvenir came back.

The Australian author Thomas Keneally visited Antarctica in 1968 as part of an official party with the United States ambassador to Australia. (The group included the ambassador's 12-year-old son, Bill Crook Jr, who became the youngest person to stand at the South Pole.) Keneally dreamed about the landscape for years afterwards. But he brought back more than dreams; at the *Discovery* hut, he picked up a Huntley and Palmers biscuit that had been left behind by one of the early expeditions.

Thomas Keneally put the biscuit on display in a glass case at his home, but after a while he started to feel it ought to go back to where he found it. Eventually he decided to return the biscuit. In 2003, he took another trip to Antarctica, this time as a tourist on board a Russian ice breaker. The funny thing was that

although he was determined to return the biscuit and had told many people he was going to, he forgot to pack it. But during the trip he met three AHT workers, and when he returned to Sydney he posted the biscuit to them. Keneally said he would never take another such souvenir and he hoped the huts would be saved and preserved so one day his grandchildren could see them too.

GETTING THERE BY AIR

Flying to Antarctica is different from flying anywhere else. The views are amazing and the runways are made of packed snow and ice. It can also take several attempts to get there.

Flights to Scott Base or McMurdo Station go from Christchurch International Airport, using Royal New Zealand Air Force C-130 Hercules and Boeing 757s or US Air Force C17s or ski-equipped C-130 Hercules aircraft. The pilots need good weather conditions to land or take off from McMurdo, so flights can often be delayed or postponed. Weather conditions can also change between taking off and landing, so once a flight leaves from Christchurch, the crew decides at the PSR (Point of Safe Return) whether or not to keep going. The PSR isn't a fixed point but depends on the type of aircraft, the amount of cargo and the wind and the weather. If the conditions aren't right, the plane heads back to Christchurch on a 'boomerang' flight.

Here's a description from the New Zealand Defence Force about what it's like to land at the Phoenix snow runway at McMurdo:

Landing on a snow runway can be tricky because it is hard to get good ground definition and contrast from the rest of the snow around it. However, because of the slightly softer nature of snow it normally makes for more pleasant landings for passengers. It has been compared to landing on a "slice of lemon-frosted sponge cake". Because the exhaust from the engines is very hot, we try to spend as little time as possible taxiing, to try to avoid melting any snow. To ensure this, we use techniques like lifting the aircraft flaps to avoid deflecting hot air on to the runway. When we land, brakes aren't very helpful because the runway is rather slippery, so we tend to use reverse thrust from the engines to slow us down.

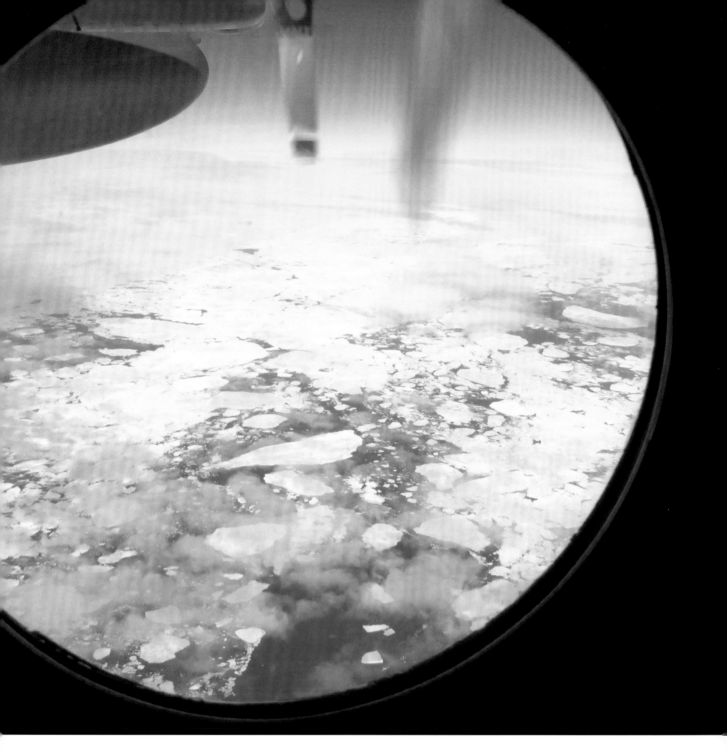

And what's it like to fly down there?

Having the opportunity to fly down to one of, if not the most remote
location in the world is definitely an honour and a privilege. On one flight
you could end up flying over the Ross Ice Shelf and seeing huge icebergs and
the apparent never-ending sea ice and then on the next flight you could fly
over the Transantarctic Mountains with incredible glaciers and 14,000-foot
mountain ranges on either side. It makes for a pretty good view out of the
office window!

Above: First view of
the sea ice from the air.
CREDIT: PHILIPPA WERRY.

SCIENCE ON THE ICE

Every summer there are about 4,000 people living and working in Antarctica as scientists or support staff. Weather conditions and the isolation make doing science on the ice different from anywhere else. Everything has to be planned in advance to make sure equipment arrives on time. If the scientists forget something, they can't pop down to the shops, so they have to be resourceful and imaginative. Instruments that work back in the lab might not operate as well in the extreme cold, so they figure out how to fix them or come up with a different way of doing things. Plans are based around a schedule of flights in and out, but the schedule often changes depending on the weather, which makes it hard to work out when people are coming or going. Sometimes people get stuck waiting for a flight, but there's nothing to be done about it. Antarctic scientists learn to be patient.

UNDER THE OCEAN

Craig Stevens is a physical oceanographer, which means he studies the physical properties and processes of the ocean, like currents, temperature and waves. He has made many trips to Antarctica to research the ocean and ice temperatures. It's important to find out as much as possible because what happens to Antarctica impacts the rest of the world.

In the Antarctic summer of 2017/18, Craig was part of a project team of hot water drillers and scientists camping on the Ross Ice Shelf, 350km from Scott Base. They lived in the middle of a huge continent for two months, but they couldn't stray far from the camp because of the danger of crevasses. Craig said, 'I've never spent so long in one place before.'

The Ross Ice Shelf is a vast area of floating ice (about the size of France or Spain) that spreads out from the glaciers of the inner polar **plateau**. The campsite sat on top of 50m of snow, above 300m of ice, and under that was 350m of ocean. Every day the ice moved about 1.6m towards the Ross Sea, so by the time they left, the camp had drifted many metres north from where it started. The floating ice plate also moves about 1.5m up and down with the movement of the tides far away in the open ocean, but the area was so vast and featureless that they couldn't feel or see this happening.

The hot water drillers used a system that melts snow in a flubber tank (like an oversized paddling pool) and heats it to about 2–4 degrees Celsius; not very warm, but much warmer than the ice below. This takes several weeks to set up, but when it's ready, a jet of hot water can melt a narrow hole through the ice

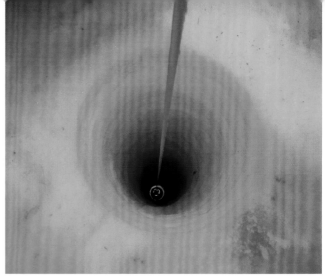

in about ten hours, and the scientists lower instruments down to measure the ocean temperatures and movement below.

It was a huge challenge for the team to bore such a deep hole, and to keep the ice from freezing the hole shut, so the previous year, they set up camp closer to Scott Base to try and work out what might go wrong. In this trial programme, equipment broke down, illness swept through the camp – putting some team members into quarantine – and the hole was only completed on the very last day, but all these experiences were welcome (except perhaps for getting sick) because they helped to iron out problems that might arise later.

As a result, everything worked much more smoothly on the actual programme in 2017/18. The hot water drillers melted a bore hole 25cm in diameter through the ice. The scientists lowered a camera and other instruments down the hole and took measurements that will help to explain how the hidden ocean underneath is warming and what that might mean for the future of the ice shelf, of Antarctica and perhaps of the whole world.

Watch more about the project:

www.youtube.com/watch?time_continue=18&v=fyjt5zpNAeg

Above right: An underwater camera travelling down the hole drilled through hundreds of metres of ice CREDIT: CRAIG STEVENS.

Below and above left: The first container camp in the ice, close to Scott Base; working out the best way to melt the snow. CREDIT: PHILIPPA WERRY.

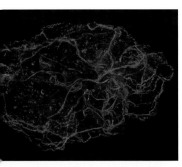

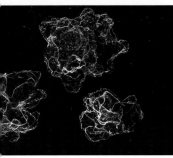

Above: Gabby photographed platelet ice under coloured light to see more detail within their structures. CREDIT: GABBY O'CONNOR.

ART ON THE ICE

Art has been part of the Antarctic story ever since painters (and later photographers) on the early ships showed the outside world what the landscape looked like. Today, many countries send writers and artists to Antarctica, and their work often helps people see the continent in a different way. Mixing art and science can also prompt the scientists to think creatively and come up with new solutions and ideas.

Gabby O'Connor, an installation artist, has been twice to Antarctica. On one of those trips, she lived for several weeks in a shipping-container camp on the ice with an oceanographic research team. The oceanographers were studying platelet ice, which forms on the underside of sea ice in different shapes and sizes, sometimes as small as a fingernail.

The exhibition that she created after this, *Studio Antarctica*, included paintings, drawings, time-lapse videos of the platelets rotating and melting and a large-scale installation showing the underside of the ice, made with the help of local school children. Gabby used packaging tape, because it is thin and can build up into layers of different shapes, and it lets the light shine through, just as light shines through to the underside of the ice.

The glowing, room-sized iceberg in another exhibition, *What Lies Beneath* was made from 3000 sheets of dyed and lacquered tissue paper fixed with 28,000 staples in shapes of triangles, kites and quadrilaterals, and suspended underneath a skylight. It is beautiful, big, strong and flimsy at the same time. In this artwork, Gabby was thinking about the life cycle of ice in Antarctica and how part of an iceberg is above the water, but most of it is hidden underneath.

Right: *What Lies Beneath*, 2011, by Gabby O'Connor. 12m x 4m x 1.5m. Tissue paper, dye, lacquer, staples, light. CREDIT: GABBY O'CONNOR, COURTESY OF THE CITY GALLERY WELLINGTON, TE WHARE TOI.

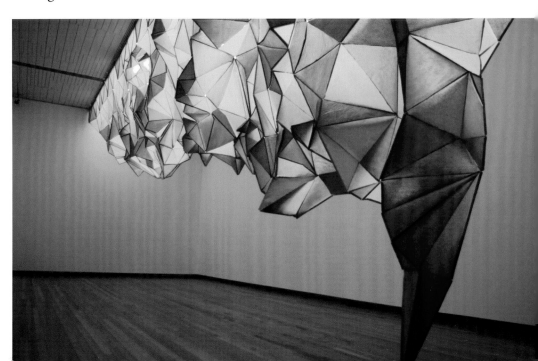

THE FIRST DANCE

In February 2018, choreographer Corey Baker and Royal New Zealand Ballet dancer Madeleine Graham created and performed 'the first dance on the earth's last great wilderness'. *Antarctica: The First Dance* took 12 days to film, in temperatures as low as minus 16°C. Even with specially designed thermal activewear, Madeleine could only work in bursts of 10–20 seconds before stopping to warm up. She practised beforehand at an ice rink, but the actual location found her abseiling down crevasses, tobogganing down a ski field, doing handstands on top of Castle Rock and dancing in front of seals.

Corey was born in Christchurch and has always been fascinated by Antarctica – he had his fifth birthday party at the International Antarctic Centre. He wanted this beautiful dance, set against a stunning backdrop of blue skies and ice, to be a celebration of the continent, but also a way to present ideas about climate change to a new audience. A message at the end of the video points out

Below: Madeleine Graham dancing on the pressure ridges in front of Scott Base. The black blobs on the ice are seals. CREDIT: MADELEINE GRAHAM IN ANTARCTICA: THE FIRST DANCE. PHOTOGRAPH JACOB BRYANT.

that 860,000 tonnes of Antarctic ice have melted in the four minutes it takes to watch.

You can see the dance on Corey's website, where he also lists ways to help slow the negative effects of climate change and describes how they used carbon offsetting to balance out the emissions that resulted from taking their project to the ice. antarctica.coreybakerdance.com

WINTER JOURNEYS

The science that gets done in Antarctica only happens because of the work of the support staff: technicians, cooks, drivers, engineers, cleaners, domestics and many others. Some staff work for all or part of the summer, and a small number stay on over winter.

Paul Lovegrove worked a summer/winter season at Scott Base as science technician and winter technical support. A vital part of his job was doing the manual weather observations every morning. These daily readings have been taken for over 60 years, since 1957, so they are a great resource in helping scientists to understand our changing climate.

Readings for wind speed and direction and atmospheric pressure are taken from instruments in the lab, but to read the minimum and maximum temperatures, and to observe cloud cover and visibility, Paul went outside to an instrument shelter called the Stevenson screen. In summer he shared the readings with the Summer Science Tech, but in winter he did nearly all of them by himself.

Below left: Paul Lovegrove, science technician and winter technical support at Scott Base, checking instruments in science lab. CREDIT: PHILIPPA WERRY.

Below right: The Stevenson screen from Scott's *Terra Nova* expedition still stands outside the Cape Evans hut. CREDIT: PHILIPPA WERRY.

I was the only person allowed to go outside during a Condition One, so I got to experience what Antarctic extreme weather is all about. When the weather is really bad, you switch on a powerful flood light from inside to make sure you don't get lost, and there's a rope to hold onto between the door and the screen. You can also use a harness to attach yourself to the rope.

Above: View of Scott Base from the pressure ridges (where the sea ice butts up against the land). The black shapes in the foreground are Weddell seals and their pups. CREDIT: PHILIPPA WERRY.

Paul also went over regularly to the Antarctica New Zealand facility at Arrival Heights, near McMurdo Station, to carry out sun ozone observations and (once a month) using the full moon. He had some spectacular drives under clear night skies, with the moon lighting the way, and sometimes an aurora. 'Other times, the wind was so strong you could hear it howling on the outside of the car, with the snow seeming to come at you horizontally.'

Arrival Heights is only 6km from Scott Base, but you still have to be very careful. 'There is an emergency kit in each of the vehicles with spare clothing, food and a sleeping bag. When leaving base, you radio in how many people are in the car and where you are going, then radio again once arrived at your destination. If you forget to do that, they'll try to contact you a few times and if there's no response, the SAR (Search And Rescue) Team will be sent out.'

Staff from McMurdo clear the road after storms, but Paul still got stuck in snow a few times and had to dig himself out. 'Another time, the weather turned bad and I couldn't get back so I ended up spending the night at Arrival Heights. I've also spent a night at McMurdo when the road back to Scott Base snowed in; winter they have a couple of dorm rooms setup as emergency crash rooms, and we did the same for the Americans at Scott Base.'

What is it like wintering over?

Winter is where all the magic happens. There are things that you never get to see anywhere else in the world: the moon, stars, aurora, the dark. Winter at Scott Base was great; everyone got on so well. McMurdo become more of a closer next-door neighbour and we joined in with a lot of their traditional celebrations. Brunch on Sunday at McMurdo was always something to look forward to. You get to know everyone a lot better over winter and it was a bit crazy when the summer staff arrived; they felt like a bunch of unwanted guests you couldn't get rid of, and it took us about a week to adjust.

Katrina Grenfell also worked a summer/winter season at Scott Base; her job as a Domestic was vital, because it's important to keep the base clean so that people don't get sick. Over summer there are about 80 people coming and going at Scott Base. In winter that number drops to a staff of 11 or 12. 'The Base becomes your home. It is like a really cool flat that you share with your flatmates and friends. You can get on with your work with much less interruption than in the summer.'

Katrina enjoyed watching the change of seasons.

During March and April the sun starts to sink lower and lower and through March you have normal days, with daytime and night-time. Then through April the sun gets lower still and the hours of daylight shrink until the sun is just peeking up over the horizon near Mt Erebus and Castle Rock for an hour or two a day, until it sets completely for 3½ months. There are some beautiful sunrises and sunsets over this time. It is like the slow sunrise turns into the slow sunset. The light is so soft and the mountains are shades of white and blue and grey pastel, and White Island and Black Island can be crimson.

What is it like wintering over?

I enjoy popping my head out the door to get a couple of breaths of fresh air and seeing what the outside looks like. Is there cloud? Is there a moon? Can you see stars? It is really cool to be able to see the Aurora. Sometimes it will be a faint light above the horizon; other times it will be beautiful graceful bands of light curling over the mountains and islands, or great pillars of light overhead.

I like to go out for a walk two or three times a week if I can. Usually just up the Hillary Trail and down the road again after work, or up Observation Hill or over to McMurdo on a day off. So long as you are dressed properly, you stay warm if you are moving. I get over to McMurdo probably about once a week, and enjoy the company of friends over there. There are always things on, whether it is a craft evening with friends, or a travel talk in the galley, or quiz night in one of the bars. We work six days a week, and Sunday is full with things like yoga, going for a walk, writing a letter, watching a movie, chatting with friends. I think it would be very hard to be bored here.

FIVE WINTERS

Agnieszka Fryckowska grew up in Auckland, not knowing much about Antarctica – but that's where she ended up. In 2004, she got a job with the British Antarctic Survey as a meteorologist at Rothera Research Station for 34 months, over two winters. Since then she has worked in several different British stations, including five winters altogether, some as station leader. In April 2016, she received the Polar Medal at Buckingham Palace for her work.

What was a typical winter day for you at Rothera?

I'd get up at 7am and have tea in the dark. I'd check the weather by looking at the machines that feed into the computer, and I'd look at the last 6–8 hours of records for trends. Then I'd take a weather balloon out of an incubator where it has been warming up for 48 hours. This helps it to be flexible and expand – by the time it bursts, it's the size of a double decker bus. I put my outdoor kit on to walk about 10 minutes away, because you can't release the balloon amongst the buildings. I did this in all weathers, and sometimes there would be seals on the runway that you couldn't see, but you could hear them and they could bite you! Then I inflated the balloon in the hangar, attached the radio instruments, calibrated it to talk to the instruments on the ground and let it go. The balloons are released at the same time all around the world.

After that, I'd have breakfast and base duties, and every three hours until midnight I'd be doing weather obs. On different days, I'd have different experiments to check. At midday I'd check the Stevenson screen. My work day finished at 5pm, except that I still had the 6pm, 9pm and midnight weather obs to do, and I also had to pass on the Ukrainian weather obs.

What was it like working down there for two winters on end?

I jumped into everything I could. There's lots to do: mountain climbing, camping in tents or igloos, going out on the sea ice or in boats, fancy dress parties, cooking, carpentry, rebuilding a skidoo. The station at Rothera sleeps

120 in summer, but large numbers go through all the time so it's more like a hotel. The winter team is only 25, so there's a special bond that forms with winterers. It's like a big family, everyone helps each other.

What would you like to tell people about Antarctica?

It's an amazing place that can teach us a lot about the planet, about climate and looking after nature. You don't have to be a scientist to get down there, you can be a plumber or a carpenter, a cook or a cleaner. It's really special and we need to look after it.

KEEPING IN TOUCH

For a long time, there was no way of communicating within Antarctica, or from Antarctica to the rest of the world. When groups set off to explore different areas, they relied on pre-planned meeting dates or notes left at depots or in huts. News and letters took months to arrive and if a ship sank in a storm after dropping off a group of men, no one would ever know where they had been left. Mawson's expedition was the first to make radio contact, but only as far as Macquarie Island.

Today, staying in touch is much easier. If you are on a base, you can email, phone and load photos on social media. But if you are out on a field camp, communication still isn't straightforward and sometimes you can feel a long way from home.

Below: Natalie's decorated noodle boxes with surprise gifts inside.
CREDIT: NATALIE ROBINSON.

Natalie Robinson is a marine physicist who studies sea ice, platelet ice and supercooled water. Every winter it gets so cold that the sea ice freezes around Antarctica. The salt leaches out of the frozen sea ice so it makes the water beneath saltier, denser and heavier. Natalie's work is to try and understand how this affects the currents and water flow in the ocean beneath the ice.

In 2016, her team used satellite phones to talk to family and friends from their field camp. They had a daily radio schedule linking up with the comms (communications) team at Scott Base, and family could phone up and ask for a message to be passed on.

> The sched has a set pattern of questions, they ask are you OK, any accidents, weather – we give a description of conditions and they give the forecast for the next few days. Then they tell us any interesting items of news, or maybe rugby scores! We build up a relationship with the person on comms and they are skilled at passing on difficult or sensitive news. In 2016 we were down there for the Kaikoura earthquake. The first we knew of it was when the 8am sched came through and after the set questions, the comms guy told us about the quake. Then he read out messages from all our families who had phoned in to let us know they were OK.

For this trip, Natalie was away from home for 4½ weeks, and she thought hard about how to keep in touch with her children.

> I boxed up little gifts in noodle boxes, covered with glow in the dark stickers, and strung them up in their bedrooms. Bedtime story-and-song time is an important ritual in our family so I recorded me reading picture books and chapter books. Every night they would have song time with my husband, then he would switch on the recording and they would look at the picture book or lie in the dark listening to the story. Even today if they pull out one of those picture books, they still remember it was the one I read to them.

Another time, Natalie set up a treasure hunt around the house with clues for each day she was away, and she bought and posted small gifts like stickers, pens and soft toys from the Scott Base shop. It isn't surprising that these are all creative ways of communication. Natalie thinks that as well as being flexible and good at problem solving, 'you have to be creative to want to do science.'

'We came back from the Barrier, telling one another we loathed the place and nothing on earth should make us return. But now the Barrier comes back to us, with its clean, open life, and the smell of the cooker, and its soft sound sleep.

– Apsley Cherry-Garrard, *The Worst Journey in the World*

THE JOURNEY HOME

It can be hard to adjust to being back in the outside world. Even returning to base from out in the field can feel strange: water flows out of a tap instead of having to be melted, there are more people, proper bathrooms with hot showers and bedrooms with comfortable beds and curtains.

Going back home can feel like even more of a culture shock. 'On the station, it's all about safety and risk assessment,' Agnieszka Fryckowska says. 'Whenever you go out, you have to get permission, tag in and out and carry the right gear and a radio, and if you're running late, you radio in before they issue a rescue party. On the Falklands, our first port of call on leaving, we'd forgotten that you could do what you wanted – you could wander off without needing to sign out! We were used to knowing everyone on the base, so we'd smile at everyone, and we gathered up our cups and plates after we'd eaten at a cafe because we were used to helping. I spent an hour in the supermarket, just looking at a weird assortment of things that I hadn't seen for two years.'

People are glad to be reunited with family and friends, and it's a treat to see birds, flowers and greenery and to have plenty of fresh fruit to eat. At the same time, they can miss their ice community, especially from the field camps where everyone relies on each other for help and support. There is something about Antarctica that gets under your skin, and some people return there over and over again.

JOURNEYS OF MEMORY

The journeys of some explorers and scientists ended in Antarctica. The first grave belongs to Nicolai Hanson, the zoologist on Borchgrevink's expedition. When the Northern Party wintered over at Cape Adare, Frank Browning collected white pebbles and used them to make a cross and write Hanson's name over his grave.

The search party who found the bodies of Scott, Wilson and Bowers buried them in their tent under a snow cairn. The tent, never seen since, is slowly drifting towards the sea with the ice. The *Terra Nova*'s carpenter made a wooden memorial cross with an inscription chosen by Cherry-Garrard: 'To strive, to seek, to find and not to yield'. The cross still sits on top of Observation Hill, between McMurdo Station and Scott Base.

Two other crosses on Ross Island remember the Heroic Age explorers. Vince's Cross sits on a headland near the *Discovery* hut. George Vince was lost early on in Scott's *Discovery* expedition when he lost his footing and shot over an icy cliff into the sea, a terrible reminder of how quickly disaster could strike. The names of Mackintosh, Hayward and Spencer-Smith, from the Ross Sea Party, are inscribed on a plaque below a wooden cross above the Cape Evans hut. The inscription is copied from a scrap of paper found years later, tucked into a copper tube lying on the snow. Another cross at Cape Denison was erected by the men still there in 1913 'to commemorate the supreme sacrifice' made by Belgrave Ninnis and Xavier Mertz 'in the cause of science'.

On a small hill behind the *Discovery* hut is a more recent memorial. The statue of the Virgin Mary, known as Our Lady of the Snows Shrine (and nicknamed Roll Cage Mary), remembers Richard T. Williams, a young driver in the US Navy who died in 1956 when his tractor fell through the sea ice while he was moving cargo to help build McMurdo Station. In 1996 the shrine was re-dedicated, not only to Williams, but also to 'all other heroic colleagues of all nations who have given their lives in order to help us better understand Antarctica and the world in which we live.'

Above left: Vince's cross, to remember George Vince who died on Scott's *Discovery* expedition. CREDIT: JANA NEWMAN, 2008–09, ANTARCTICA NEW ZEALAND PICTORIAL COLLECTION.

Below left: Memorial Plaque for cross on Windvane Hill above Cape Evans, to remember the three men who died from the Ross Sea Party. CREDIT: PHOTOGRAPHER UNKNOWN, NO DATE, ANTARCTICA NEW ZEALAND PICTORIAL COLLECTION.

Left: Our Lady of the Snows Shrine, near McMurdo Station. Also known as Roll Cage Mary, after the metal grid that surrounds the figure of Mary to protect it from rocks that might be hurled around in storms; a roll cage is a protective frame in a vehicle. CREDIT: PHILIPPA WERRY.

Above left: Hanson's cross, the first grave in Antarctica. CREDIT: LAWRIE CAIRNS, 1972–73, ANTARCTICA NEW ZEALAND PICTORIAL COLLECTION.

Top right: Snow cairn over the bodies of Scott, Wilson and Bowers. CREDIT: AUSTRALIAN NATIONAL MARITIME MUSEUM [ANMM COLLECTION 00053989] / FLICKR COMMONS.

Above right: Prayer flags on Observation Hill. CREDIT: PHOTOGRAPHER UNKNOWN, 2006–07, ANTARCTICA NEW ZEALAND PICTORIAL COLLECTION.

TOURISM JOURNEYS

Lars-Eric Lindblad, born in Sweden, emigrated to America and set up a firm called Lindblad Travel to take people to remote parts of the world. He ran the first tourist cruise to the Antarctic Peninsula in January 1966 on a chartered Argentinian naval ship. There were no rules back then about keeping a distance from wildlife and Mrs Bessie Sweeney, aged 86, said the highlight of her trip was 'holding a penguin in my arms, stroking his chest and observing him relax and even enjoy being petted.' (*Antarctic*, v 4 no 6 June 1966)

Lindblad later took his own ship, the *Lindblad Explorer*, and used small inflatable boats called Zodiacs to get passengers ashore. He ran the first tourist trips to McMurdo Sound in 1968 on the *Magga Dan*. His tours were educational as well as adventurous and he encouraged people to learn about and appreciate the environment.

Today's tourists mostly travel on cruise ships to the Antarctic Peninsula over the summer season from November to March. Any landings must be booked in advance with the International Association of Antarctica Tour Operators (IAATO). There are specific requirements for visiting historic sites, and cruise ship operators must keep to IAATO Wildlife Watching Guidelines, for example:

- No more than 100 people ashore at a time, plus guides
- Keep at least 5m from penguins
- Keep at least 15m from fur seals and sea lions
- Walk slowly and carefully
- Give wildlife the right of way
- Keep to flagged routes
- Remove all rubbish at end of trip

IAATO also keeps count of tourist ships and passengers. In the 2017–18 season, 51,707 people visited the Antarctic Peninsula, up 17% from the year before. This is a tiny number compared to other parts of the world, but people still disagree over whether tourists should be allowed to visit Antarctica at all.

No:

- In the past, tourist ships have run aground or collided with icebergs and passengers had to be rescued.
- There's always a risk of accidents and of pollution, from oil spills to plastic bags that blow away in the wind.
- Some tourists ignore the IAATO guidelines, or don't watch where they are walking, and it's easy to damage the landscape.
- Cruise ships create high levels of greenhouse gas emissions (this also applies to the flights needed to transport scientists, support staff, equipment and food for the summer season).

Yes:

- Lindblad's motto was 'you can't protect what you don't know.' Tourism creates 'Antarctic ambassadors' who go back home wanting to help protect the Antarctic environment and wildlife.

Below: King penguin chick in sleet, Salisbury Plain, South Georgia. CREDIT: KATJA RIEDEL.

Above: Passengers on a Zodiac cruise observe a Weddell seal on an ice floe with the expedition ship in the background, Antarctic Peninsula. CREDIT: KATJA RIEDEL.

Below: Gentoo (left) and Adélie penguin, at Brown Bluff on the northern tip of the Antarctic Peninsula. CREDIT: KATJA RIEDEL.

Katja's second home

Katja Riedel has been to the Antarctic so many times that it's like a second home. On her first trip, she overwintered at the German research station, Neumayer, with eight other people. Her job was to look after the Atmospheric Observatory, and since then she's worked at other stations like Casey and Scott Base, measuring ozone, drilling ice cores and taking samples of 120,000-year-old ice.

Nowadays, Katja is a lecturer and guide on tourist ships that set off from Ushuaia in Tierra del Fuego, Argentina. From here, it's about 40 hours sailing time to the Antarctic Peninsula. These trips are expensive, but for some people it's a lifelong dream and they save up for years to afford it. Everyone on board has a special reason for wanting to go. Penguins are top of most people's lists, as well as seeing whales and orca, icebergs and the historic huts.

During the trip across the stormy Drake Passage, Katja gives talks on subjects like glaciers, ice cores, penguins and climate change. Once they reach the Antarctic Peninsula, she takes groups of tourists ashore on Zodiacs. Katja helps passengers off the ship, drives the Zodiac through icy waters, monitors the weather and landing conditions, marks the walking tracks with flags, repeats the

rules about respecting the environment and wildlife, makes sure the passengers are warm and safe, and explains what they are looking at.

Katja's favourite place on these trips is South Georgia. The scenery is amazing and it teems with wildlife: different species of seals, penguins, and albatrosses, all in their natural habitat. At St Andrews Bay, half a million king penguins gather in huge colonies to raise their fluffy brown chicks.

AIR NEW ZEALAND FLIGHT 901

When two airlines – Qantas and Air New Zealand – started sightseeing flights in the 1970s, it seemed an opportunity not to be missed. These were long, 12 to 14-hour flights, but the time quickly passed with food and drink, guest commentaries and plenty of photo opportunities, and people raved about the experience. Two people even got married on a Qantas flight, and everyone on board had a slice of wedding cake and glass of champagne.

Early on the morning of 28 November 1979, Air New Zealand Flight 901 set off from Auckland to McMurdo Sound. It had 22 crew on board and 237 passengers from New Zealand, Australia, Britain, the United States, Japan, Canada, France and Switzerland.

After about four hours of flying, the airplane was in touch with air traffic control at McMurdo. When radio contact was lost, McMurdo staff feared something was wrong. Search and rescue efforts began with other aircraft and helicopters. Air New Zealand officials gave briefings as worried relatives waited for news. By 10pm, they knew that the fuel would have run out. It wasn't until midnight that wreckage was found strewn across the icy slopes where the plane had slammed into the side of Mt Erebus. There were no survivors.

The operation to examine the site and recover and later identify the bodies was a grim and gruelling task including abseiling into crevasses and collecting passports, cameras, watches and personal possessions. Air New Zealand, the Chief Inspector of Air Accidents and the Judge who led the Royal Commission of Enquiry disagreed about what caused the disaster, and even today people hold different opinions as to what was the cause.

Above: A wooden cross was built at Scott Base and put in place at Mt Erebus just before Christmas 1979. A Japanese scientist who went with the memorial party sprinkled sake on the cross and buried at its base a scroll listing the names of the 24 Japanese who died in the crash. CREDIT: PHOTOGRAPHER UNKNOWN, 1979–80, ANTARCTICA NEW ZEALAND PICTORIAL COLLECTION.

Peter Mulgrew, one of Hillary's tractor team to the South Pole, later went climbing with Hillary in the Himalayas. Mulgrew got terribly sick near the summit of Mt Makalu and had to be carried most of the way down by Sherpa porters. He was lucky to survive but lost both feet and a hand to frostbite. Mulgrew and Hillary both acted as onboard commentators for the Air New Zealand sightseeing flights, but it was Mulgrew who was on board Flight 901, and he was killed along with everyone else when the plane crashed.

CHAPTER THREE

Animal journeys

Antarctic animals like whales, penguins, seals and seabirds carry out their own amazing journeys. (But not polar bears. There are no polar bears in Antarctica, and no sharks, either.)

Big and small

Humpback whales
Humpback whales are enormous, powerful and as agile as acrobats. They can swim on their backs or on their sides, hop along the waves with just their head showing or burst right out of the water and crash back down in an explosion of bubbles, spray and foam. Humpbacks are also great travellers. Their journey

Below: Humpback mother and calf at Hawaii, Maui, Hawaiian Is. CREDIT: IMAGE ID: SANC0612, NOAA'S SANCTUARIES COLLECTION, NOAA PHOTO LIBRARY. THIS WORK IS LICENSED UNDER A CREATIVE COMMONS ATTRIBUTION 2.0 GENERIC LICENSE.

is one of the longest migration journeys of any mammal in the world.

The humpbacks that live in the Southern Ocean have a thick layer of blubber under their skin to protect them against the frigid temperatures. They spend the summer feeding on krill, which flourish in the cold Antarctic waters. In autumn, they travel for about 5000km from their icy southern home to the tropical Pacific Ocean. They don't eat on their journey. Sometimes they stop and rest for a while. Then they set off again, always heading north.

After weeks of swimming, the whales reach their winter home, where the baby whales (called calves) are born. Next to the adult whales they look tiny, but they are already four meters long. Every day they drink hundreds of litres of their mother's milk. In autumn, when the calves are several months old, the whales set off back to their southern home. Sometimes they swim in pods, sometimes alone. The adult whales pause now and then to eat, but they are too hungry to stop for long. Their throats are narrow and they can't swallow big fish. They have hardly eaten for months and they are waiting to gorge on swarms of krill.

Other breeding populations of humpback whales travel south for almost the same distance from Alaska to Hawaii. Some whales have been tagged so their movements can be traced across the ocean, but nobody knows for certain why their long migrations occur. The calves have no protective layer of blubber, so one reason might be that they need to give birth in warmer climates.

Krill

Antarctic krill are tiny – only about 6cm long and a gram in weight – but there are so many of them that their total weight is estimated to be more than the weight of all the people on earth. Krill feed on small floating plants and algae that live under the sea ice, and in turn they provide food for seals, penguins, seabirds, fish and whales. They form a vital part of the Antarctic food chain. Blue whales, the largest animals ever to have lived, survive almost entirely on krill; one blue whale can eat up to four tons of krill every day.

Left: Krill are a vital part of the undersea food chain. Despite being so tiny, they can travel for hundreds of kilometres through the ocean. CREDIT: MALCOLM MACFARLANE, 1989–90, ANTARCTICA NEW ZEALAND PICTORIAL COLLECTION.

Right: Red sea stars (*Odontaster validus*), some of the beautiful, delicate undersea creatures in Antarctic waters. CREDIT: ROD BUDD, 2001–02, ANTARCTICA NEW ZEALAND PICTORIAL COLLECTION.

Krill have to swim constantly to stay afloat. They gather in swarms that spread for kilometres and are tens of metres deep. The swarms colour the sea red or orange and can be so enormous that they are visible from space. Despite these huge swarms, scientists have recorded big drops in the number of Antarctic krill over the last 40 years. Nobody knows for certain why this is, but it may be related to loss of habitat. Krill need sea ice for shelter and to eat the ice-algae, so if the ocean gets warmer and the sea ice melts, it may affect krill numbers. Because they are so important in the Antarctic food chain, that will have an impact on other wildlife as well.

THE INVASION OF THE KING CRABS

On the ocean floor off the Antarctic coast live beautiful undersea creatures such as sponges, sea anemones, ribbon worms, brittlestars, sea urchins, sea lilies and sea spiders. The water here is too cold for most predators. Most of the fish species don't have strong jaws to prey on them and until recently there have been no crabs. As a result, these creatures have evolved without any protective coverings (like harder shells or skeletons), because they haven't needed them. Many of them are delicate and brittle, and they can grow to a great size.

King crabs live further out in the deep ocean. The cold water has stopped them from coming any closer to land, but climate change means that the shallow waters in the continental shelf are getting warmer. Scientists have sent down undersea cameras into the water off the western Antarctic Peninsula and found colonies of king crabs living there, and it's possible they have been there for some time unnoticed. If the water keeps getting warmer, there will be nothing to stop the king crabs advancing and the undersea creatures will have no defences against their crushing claws.

SEALS FAR FROM THE SEA

The Dry Valleys, west of McMurdo Sound, are sometimes compared to the surface of the planet Mars; in fact, **NASA** engineers have tested equipment there to be used on Mars. It hasn't rained there for two million years, but there are lakes and streams that are fed by snow melt from glaciers.

Another unusual feature of the Dry Valleys is that scientists have found remains of crabeater, Weddell and leopard seals, mummified in the dry climate, some of them hundreds of years old. Men from the *Discovery*, *Nimrod* and *Terra Nova* all noticed these remains, and a Victoria University of Wellington expedition in 1958–59 counted 99 seal carcasses, up to 45 miles inland.

Seals are fast and graceful swimmers but clumsy out of the water. Why would they make their way inland into such a steep, rocky area? Do they simply get lost? When the sledging party from the *Discovery* found a mummified seal carcass high up on a glacier, Scott wrote, 'it grows more than ever wonderful how these creatures can have got so far from the sea. We never satisfactorily explained this matter.' Even today, nobody knows for certain.

In 1990, Dr Diane McKnight, from the University of Colorado, was working with a team of scientists in the Dry Valleys. Diane is a limnologist, which means she studies lakes, rivers and streams. The team was collecting water samples and measuring water flow when they came across something strange: a trail in a patch of snow, but no footprints. One of the team went to investigate what was making the trail and found a Weddell seal pup.

The scientists knew it must be hungry, because there was nothing to eat except snow, but there are strict rules about how to deal with wildlife and they couldn't feed it. Some seal scientists identified it from a flipper tag as belonging to a seal colony in McMurdo Sound. They painted an orange stripe down its back for identification and then left it alone.

A few days later, the seal pup turned up at the scientists' campsite and this time they felt they had to try and save it. They made a bed of blankets over a sheet of wood on top of a cargo net, then guided the seal pup onto the blankets and strapped it in. The net was hitched up to a helicopter and the baby seal was flown, slung under the helicopter, back to the sea ice to rejoin the other seals.

The scientists named some streams in the area where they were working, and one stream is now called Lost Seal Stream to remember the first time that a live seal was found in the Dry Valleys.

Penguin journeys

How to count penguins

The Ross Sea region has about one third of the worldwide population of Adélie penguins: over one million breeding pairs in 38 colonies. They breed on land, on nests of stones and rocks, and usually return to the same spot every year.

A penguin census has been done on Ross Island almost every year since 1981. It takes place in late November or early December, when one parent bird is sitting on the eggs and the other is out at sea feeding (both parents take turns looking after the chicks). That makes it possible to calculate the number of breeding pairs.

When Pamela Young went to Cape Bird in 1969–70, they counted the penguins manually and she found it as boring as housework, but today's counting is done based on photos taken out of a helicopter. A pilot flies above the penguin colony at a set minimum height (so as not to disturb the birds), while someone leans out the door and takes hundreds of photos of the ground beneath. The photos are fitted together like a jigsaw puzzle and counted using digital technology that can tell the difference between a group of penguins and a clump of rocks.

Factors like weather, the thickness and extent of the sea ice, the amount of

Below: An aerial view of the Adélie penguin colony, taken during the penguin count at Cape Adare. All the dark splotches are groups of penguins. Borchgrevink's hut is on the middle left-hand side of the image. CREDIT: FIONA SHANHUN.

krill in the ocean and commercial fishing can all affect the penguin population. Changes in penguin numbers can act like a signal to show environmental and climate change. That's why it's so important to have accurate numbers that can be compared from one year to the next.

HAPPY FEET

Emperor penguins are the largest of all the penguin species. They can dive the deepest (500m) and stay under the longest. They breed on the ice, in winter, without nests; the female passes the egg to the male and then goes to sea to feed, while the male balances the egg on his feet, protected by a special feathered pouch. The males huddle together to keep warm and may go for months without eating while waiting for the females to return.

Young emperor penguins spend the first years of their lives living amongst the floating sea ice. Some swim beyond that into the Southern Ocean, or even further.

In June 2011, a woman walking her dog along the beach at Peka Peka on the Kapiti coast north of Wellington noticed something white on the sand. It was an emperor penguin, a long way from home. Only one emperor penguin had ever been seen in New Zealand before, at Oreti Beach, near Invercargill, in April 1967. That penguin was released at sea the next day off Foveaux Strait.

The penguin at Peka Peka was nicknamed Happy Feet by the crowds who flocked to see it. Department of Conservation workers and Peka Peka locals watched over it, making sure that reporters, TV crews and onlookers didn't get too close. They hoped it would return to the sea, but after four days it started to eat sticks and wet sand, perhaps thinking that the sand was snow.

Happy Feet was taken to The Nest Te Kōhanga (the

A group of penguins is called a colony, but it can also be called a raft (on the water), a waddle, rookery, parcel, huddle or a creche (for penguin chicks).

Left: Happy Feet being cared for at Wellington Zoo.
CREDIT: WELLINGTON ZOO.

animal hospital) in Wellington Zoo. Tests showed that he was male and X-rays under anaesthetic showed a mass of sand in his stomach and throat. The sand was flushed out of his system and zoo staff kept him in a special room on a bed of ice, feeding him on whole salmon and letting him swim in an outdoor pool in cold weather. Meanwhile penguin experts got together to work out what to do next. Taking him back to Antarctica would be too difficult. There was a lot of public debate about his future, and whether he should be kept permanently at the zoo.

At the end of August, Happy Feet was microchipped and fitted with a satellite tracking device, put into a crate and loaded on board the **NIWA** ship *Tangaroa*, which was heading south on a research trip. A Wellington Zoo vet and NIWA staff looked after him until, on 4 September, Happy Feet was released into the Southern Ocean near Campbell Island, 1250km south from where he came ashore at Peka Peka Beach.

People around the world followed Happy Feet's story, leaving hundreds of online comments and queries. The tag showed that he swam about 113km in a south easterly direction over the next five days. After that no more signals were received. The transmitter might have fallen off or been damaged, or something might have happened to Happy Feet, but we will probably never know.

Watch Happy Feet's release here: www.niwa.co.nz/videos/happy-feet-release

Below left and right: Happy Feet being released into the Southern Ocean from NIWA's research vessel *Tangaroa*.
CREDIT: NATIONAL INSTITUTE OF WATER AND ATMOSPHERIC RESEARCH (NIWA).

SHIPS' CATS

The early explorers took cats to keep down the mice and rats on their ships. Litters of kittens were born on board. Some ships' cats returned home safely, but cold weather and dangerous conditions meant that others were drowned or lost at sea.

One of the sailors on the *Belgica* had a kitten called Nansen, after the Norwegian explorer. The kitten was a general favourite, 'happy and contented, and glad to be petted and loved by everyone', but the long dark winter affected him too. Frederick Cook recorded that his mood became one of 'growling discontent ... We have showered upon him our affections, but the long darkness has made him turn against us.' When Nansen the kitten died, they were glad he was out of his misery but they all missed him.

One of the best-known Antarctic cats is Mrs Chippy, a tabby cat belonging to Harry McNeish, ship's carpenter on the *Endurance*. 'Chippy' is a slang term for a carpenter, and 'Mrs' Chippy was later found to be a male, but the name stuck.

Mrs Chippy was nimble and sure-footed, and used to climb the rigging, as Frank Worsley noted, 'exactly after the manner of a seaman going aloft'. He was a favourite with many of the crew, especially Perce Blackborow, a 19-year-old who came aboard as a stowaway. When the *Endurance* was trapped in the ice, Mrs Chippy stayed on board because he didn't like the feel of ice under his paws, but eventually the crew had to abandon ship. Shackleton knew if they were to survive, they could only take what was absolutely essential. On 29 October 1915, he wrote in his diary: 'This afternoon Sallie's three youngest pups, Sue's Sirius, and Mrs. Chippy, the carpenter's cat, have to be shot. We could not undertake the maintenance of weaklings under the new conditions. Macklin, Crean, and the carpenter seemed to feel the loss of their friends rather badly.'

Below left: Iggy the cat came to Antarctica in the pocket of an American sailor, but she wasn't allowed onto the US Navy base and was adopted by the cook at Scott Base instead. Named Iggy (after the IGY), she spent a year down south before being flown back to Christchurch the following summer. CREDIT: BRIAN SANDFORD, 1958–59, ANTARCTICA NEW ZEALAND PICTORIAL COLLECTION.

Below and below right: Close up of plaque and statue of Mrs Chippy in Karori cemetery, lying on the grave of her owner Harry McNeish. CREDIT: DAVID WERRY.

Mrs Chippy was fussed over in his last hours and given a special meal of sardines, his favourite food. Shackleton's orders had to be obeyed, but Harry McNeish was very sad to lose Mrs Chippy. McNeish later moved to New Zealand, where he died penniless in 1930. The Navy organised a funeral for him and in 2004, the New Zealand Antarctic Society paid for a life-size bronze statue of Mrs Chippy to be put on top of his grave.

THE DOGS

> To drive by dog-team over the frozen sea, in the crisp Polar air, is one of the most exhilarating experiences imaginable … The rush of the keen air into one's face; the swish of the sledge-runners, and the sound of forty paws pat-a-pat-a-patting on the crackling snow, is something that cannot be described. It must be experienced.   (Ponting, *The Great White South*)

Sledge dogs were originally different breeds of huskies from the Arctic regions of Siberia, Greenland and northern Canada, and the first ones came to Antarctica with Carsten Borchgrevink. Huskies were easy to feed because they ate seal meat (unlike the ponies, whose food had to be brought by ship and carried on the sledges). They were strong and tough and had thick coats and bushy tails to help them cope with the cold. In blizzards they would lie curled up under a covering of snow. When the *Endurance* was stuck in the ice, the men built 'dogloos' as kennels, and chained the dogs up by burying the chain in the snow, under chunks of ice, and pouring water over to cement it in.

Dogs and puppies were an important part of Antarctic life. As well

Right: Sculptor Mark Whyte created this statue of a sled dog in Lyttleton. Local school children were invited to name him and 'Hector' was the winning entry. The plaque says the statue 'celebrates the contribution of Lyttelton to exploration in Antarctica and the Southern Ocean' and symbolises 'the courage, commitment and comradeship of all those involved'.
CREDIT: DAVID WERRY.

as pulling sledges, they provided friendship and companionship. Even when planes and tractors were introduced, some people still preferred dog teams. But under the Antarctic Treaty, it was decided that no non-native species should be allowed in Antarctica, and the dogs had to go. The last dogs left from the British station of Rothera in February 1994.

TARO AND JIRO

The Japanese Antarctic Research Program (JARE) set up a base at Syowa Station in January 1957 as part of the IGY. The expedition included 11 men and 15 dogs; specially trained Sakhalin huskies (in Japanese, *Karafuto-ken*). The men were to be replaced by a second team, but the ice breaker bringing them sailed into a huge storm and couldn't reach Syowa Station. The first team, running low on supplies, had to be rescued by helicopter. They left the dogs behind with food for several days, hoping to come back for them after the storm, but it was too dangerous to return.

A year later, the third team arrived at Syowa Station. They found that seven of the dogs had died near the station. The other eight had escaped, and nobody expected to see them again. But suddenly two of them appeared, bounding towards the newcomers: brothers Taro and Jiro, the youngest of the dogs. They had survived eleven months on their own, probably by learning to hunt penguins and seals.

Taro and Jiro became national heroes and their dog breed was the most popular in Japan for decades. Jiro stayed at Syowa Station and died in 1960. Toro went back to Sapporo, his home, and lived at Hokkaido University. Their story was told in the 1983 Japanese film *Nankyoku Monogatari* (called *Antarctica* outside of Japan) and a Disney movie, *Eight Below*.

OTHER FAMOUS ANTARCTIC DOGS

Obersten ('the colonel') was one of the lead dogs on Amundsen's trek to the South Pole. He returned to Norway and lived the rest of his life with Oscar Wisting's family in Horten. Everyone in town knew him, butchers gave him large chunks of meat and he was treated as a local celebrity.

Igloo (Iggy for short), a white fox terrier with one brown ear, was found as a stray puppy in Washington DC. He went with Admiral Byrd to the North Pole, Antarctica and on a flight over the South Pole. Igloo felt the cold more than the huskies and wore a jacket, trousers and fur-lined boots made by the ship's sailmaker. He joined Admiral Byrd for ticker tape parades in New York and Boston and met many important people, including Presidents Hoover and Coolidge. He was even given a gold medal by the Tail Waggers Club of New York. When he died in 1931, children from around the world wrote to tell Byrd how sorry they were.

Osman was one of about 30 huskies brought from Siberia for Scott's second expedition. On the *Terra Nova* the dogs were chained to the deck and exposed to the elements. During one storm, Osman's chain broke and he was washed overboard. Luckily the next wave washed him back. Osman was once lead dog when all the other dogs on the team fell into a crevasse and he kept his footing

Below: Huskies at Scott Base.
CREDIT: RICHARD MCBRIDE, 1964–65, ANTARCTICA NEW ZEALAND PICTORIAL COLLECTION.

and held the rope until they were all rescued. After the expedition, Osman was presented to Wellington Zoo, to be joined later by Oscar (from Shackleton's Ross Sea Party) and Jacko, a monkey brought back from Egypt and France by World War One troops.

THE PONIES

Scott and Shackleton took ponies as well as dogs. The ponies had a miserable time on the ships. They were cold and wet and struggled to keep their footing in the storms. At Cape Evans, they lived in stables built against the side of the hut. Titus Oates, a keen horseman, thought Scott's ponies were badly chosen, old and not very strong, but he and the Russian groom, Anton Omelchenko, spent hours out in the stables, looking after them with care and devotion.

All the ponies had their own distinct personalities. Christopher was bad-tempered and it often took three or four men to harness him.

Cherry-Garrard described some of the others:

> There were the steady workers like Punch and Nobby; there were one or two definitely weak ponies like Blossom, Blücher and Jehu; and there were one or two strong but rather impossible beasts. One of these was soon known as Weary Willie … A brief acquaintance soon convinced me that he was without doubt a cross between a pig and a mule.

Scott took eleven ponies when he set out for the Pole. The ponies could pull heavy loads but they struggled in deep snow drifts and their sweat turned to freezing layers of ice on their thick coats; at the end of every march, the men had to spend extra time brushing the ponies down, covering them with blankets and building snow walls to shelter them. The ponies battled on but Scott knew that they wouldn't be able to make their way up the steep glacier that led to the polar plateau. At that point the remaining ponies had to be killed. The men had grown fond of them and it was a horrible task. From then on, Scott and his men pulled the sledges by themselves.

Watch Scott, Wilson and the pony Nobby here: www.youtube.com/watch?v=3aFUAsrrI48

NAMES IN THE SKY

Colonel Ronnie Smith spent 30 years in the US Air Force, many of them in Antarctica. He wanted to find a way to honour the dogs and ponies that worked so hard for the early explorers, so he looked to the skies. Colonel Smith's idea was to re-name the waypoints on the flight path to Antarctica after Scott's ponies and Shackleton's dogs.

Waypoints make up a grid of fixed points all over the world, located by latitude and longitude. Pilots use them to keep to their routes or to figure out when to change altitude or direction. The waypoints are churned out by computers in five-letter sequences. Most are not actual words, but they must be easy to pronounce.

There are 12 waypoints between Christchurch and McMurdo. One is BYRRD, for Admiral Byrd, but Ronnie Smith proposed changing the other eleven. He persuaded the United States Air Force, air traffic control, embassies and other authorities to agree, and then decided on eleven animals and worked out a five-letter variation of their names. The new waypoint names were introduced in 2010, in time for the centenary of Amundsen reaching the Pole.

These are the animals that he chose:

Scott's ponies		Amundsen's dogs	
Snippets	SNIPT	Per	PEHRR
Jimmy Pigg	JIPIG	Helge	HELGE
Bones	BOENZ	Lasse	LASSE
Jehu	JEHOO	Mylius	MYLUS
Nobby	NOBEY	Fritjof	FRITH
		Uroa	URROA

No ponies made it to the Pole, but all of these dogs did.

NAMES ON THE GROUND

In 2017, the Australian Antarctic Division Place Names Committee announced that 26 landmarks would be named after the huskies that went with Mawson on the *Aurora*. The place names include:

- Pavlova Island (the dog Pavlova was named by Begrave Ninnis after the dancer Anna Pavlova, a friend of his)
- Switzerland Island (Switzerland was named after Xavier Mertz's home country)
- Ginger Reef (Ginger had a reddish-golden coat)
- Castor Rock (Castor died in the crevasse with Ninnis)
- Devil Rock (Devil was a very bad-tempered dog)
- Blizzard Island (Blizzard was a pup named after the bad weather at Cape Denison)

A PERFECT FARMYARD

Cats, dogs and ponies were not the only animals to be taken south. Tom Crean brought a pet rabbit on board the *Terra Nova*. Scott recorded that it gave birth to 17 baby rabbits on Christmas Day, 'and Crean has given away 22! I don't know what will become of the parent or family; at present they are warm and snug enough, tucked away in the fodder under the forecastle.'

Cherry-Garrard commented that it was like 'a perfect farmyard' at Cape Evans, with ponies and dogs on land, penguins wandering up to look at them, skua overhead, seals on the ice and a blue Persian kitten, rabbits and squirrels on the ship. 'The whole place teems with life,' he wrote.

When Admiral Byrd went down to Antarctica in 1933, he took three Guernsey cows, partly to provide fresh milk, but also for publicity purposes. His plan worked; Klondike, already pregnant, gave birth to a calf on the way south. The calf was named Iceberg and became a media sensation; back in America, Iceberg was treated to 'hay cocktails' (hay with cracked ice) in hotel ballrooms. Finne Ronne's 1947 expedition, which included his wife and Jennie Darlington, enjoyed fresh eggs from five hens, which they donated to a British team when they left. Today, under the Antarctic Treaty, no non-native animals are allowed in Antarctica.

CHAPTER FOUR

THE LANDSCAPE

FOSSILS: CLUES TO THE PAST

Edward Wilson found some fossils on the way back from the South Pole with Scott. 'Wilson, with his sharp eyes, has picked several plant impressions,' Scott wrote on 8 February 1912. The men loaded the rocks onto the sledges and dragged them all the way to their last campsite, determined not to throw them out, even when they were getting weaker and weaker.

Today we know that the Antarctic continent itself has shifted over millions of years, and the proof for this lies in fossils, which show petrified remains of plants and animals that once lived there.

Ted Daeschler is a paleontologist at the Academy of Natural Sciences at Drexel University, Philadelphia, and he studies fossils for clues about what the environment and climate used to be like. Over the 2016/17 Antarctic summer, he spent three weeks camping with a team of American and Australian scientists in the Dry Valleys. This is an ideal place for fossil research because it is mostly free of ice and the fossils can be seen embedded in the exposed rocks.

Each day, the team set out from their campsite to hunt for fossil sites in layers of rock called Aztec Siltstone. When they found a layer of rocks with fossils visible in it, they used simple hand tools – chisels, a rock hammer and brushes – to investigate and excavate them. The fossils might be as large as a dinner plate or as small as a pinhead; they might be a single shark tooth, or a complete individual of an armored fish.

Below left: John Long, an Australian palaeontologist, was part of the same fossil hunting team as Ted Daeschler in 2016/17. Here he is with the tools of the trade and a fossil discovery at Aztec Mountain, January 2017. CREDIT: JOHN LONG, FLINDERS UNIVERSITY
Below right: Leaf fossils dating back 15 million years, to the time when small beech trees grew in the Dry Valleys. Tim Naish, a glaciologist from Victoria University of Wellington, showed these to me at Scott Base. It was almost unbelievable to think they were so old. CREDIT: PHILIPPA WERRY

The scientists then wrapped the rocks up with plenty of padding, labelled them carefully and stored them back at the campsite in large plastic buckets with lids. Eventually these fossil discoveries were shipped to the United States from McMurdo Station. Back at the museum, the fossils were unwrapped and catalogued to form part of the museum's collection.

These were fossils of aquatic vertebrates (fish and other sea creatures with backbones) from the Middle Devonian age, 385 million years ago, long before the first dinosaurs. Their presence embedded in the rocks helps to build up a picture of what the world was like hundreds of millions of years ago, when all the continents were in different places from where they are today. Scientists can compare these fossil samples found in the Dry Valleys to other similar samples of the same age, found in places like Australia and South Africa, when they were part of the same ancient landmass.

Other fossil discoveries show us that more recently, but still millions of years ago, forests of beech and other trees flourished and – yes – there were dinosaurs in Antarctica.

ICE AND ICEBERGS

Ice covers 98% of Antarctica. Some is on land, like the ice sheet that smothers the continent, up to 2.2km thick, or glacier ice with its deep crevasses. Some is at sea, like floating pack ice or pancake ice. In between are the ice shelves, like the Ross Ice Shelf, which cascade down from the glaciers and float on the sea but are solid enough to travel over.

The ice on land is always moving, gradually sliding over thousands of years from the mountains down to the sea. This is why the Geographic South Pole marker has to be shifted every year.

Above left: New Geographic South Pole marker being unveiled on 1 January 2009. This marker was made by South Pole winter staff member David Postler. CREDIT: TAKEN BY REINHART PIUK. UNITED STATES ANTARCTIC PROGRAM / NATIONAL SCIENCE FOUNDATION.

Above right: The 2012 Geographic South Pole marker was created by South Pole winter machinist Steele Diggles. It depicts Amundsen's team at the South Pole on one side, and Scott's team on the other side. CREDIT: TAKEN BY KATIE HESS. UNITED STATES ANTARCTIC PROGRAM / NATIONAL SCIENCE FOUNDATION.

There are two Pole markers at the South Pole. The ceremonial one, where official photographs are taken, is a striped post with a shiny metal globe, surrounded by flags of the countries that signed the original Antarctic Treaty. But because the ice moves about 10m each year, this no longer marks the true position of the Geographic South Pole. Surveyors work out the actual position and on 1 January every year, a new pole marker is put in place, created by the winter-over crew at Amundsen-Scott South Pole Station. The design of the new marker is kept secret until the unveiling ceremony. For a very short time, it will be in the right spot, but within a day, the moving ice will have carried it a few centimetres away.

On land, the crevasses in the ice are a constant danger. At sea, the ice can trap ships for days or months, and is strong enough to crush and destroy them, as happened to the *Endurance*. Icebergs can be enormous, like floating mountains, and will plough through anything in their way.

Icebergs usually stay south of the Antarctic Circumpolar Current (a swirling current that circles the continent) but wind and waves can take them further north. In November 2006, a flotilla of icebergs reached the Otago coastline near Dunedin. People bought tickets for sightseeing trips on helicopters and Air New Zealand diverted some flights to fly over them. News teams landed on them. Shrek the famous merino sheep was shorn on an iceberg to raise money for charity. But a planned iceberg wedding was cancelled because it might have been unsafe, and not a legal wedding.

THE METEORITE HUNTERS

A meteorite is a rock that plummets to Earth from outer space. Finding meteorites is like exploring outer space without a spaceship. Many come from the asteroid belt between the orbits of Mars and Jupiter, but others come from the moon or Mars, and they can be millions or billions of years old.

Meteorites fall at random, but more have been found in Antarctica than anywhere else in the world. The cold and dry conditions preserve them, they stand out against the ice and the movement of the ice tends to channel them into certain areas. The first meteorite was found in 1912 by members of Mawson's expedition. Japanese and Russian geologists found more in the 1960s. William Cassidy, an American geology professor, was intrigued by this and helped set up a program called the Antarctic Search for Meteorites, or ANSMET. Since 1976, more than 23,000 meteorites have been collected.

Every year, volunteers apply to join the ANSMET field season. When they find a meteorite they photograph it, carefully bag it with tongs and note the location with GPS coordinates. The meteorites are sent to the NASA Johnson Space Center in Houston, Texas, to be weighed and classified. After that, they are preserved in dry nitrogen storage cabinets in the Smithsonian Institution meteorite library in Suitland, Maryland, and the librarians loan out samples to scientists around the world for their research.

One of the volunteers in the 2017–18 season was Juliane Gross from Rutgers University, New Jersey. With three other people in Team A (for Awesome), she camped at 2600m at Mt Cecily, named by Shackleton after his daughter. Their first task every morning was to light the stove to warm the tent up. It took

Below left: Juliane in front of a meteorite with a counter, ready to tag it (every meteorite gets a unique number).

Below right: Juliane holding the biggest meteorite of the season. Some meteorites were as big as rugby balls, others were as small as marbles.
CREDIT BOTH: JULIANE GROSS, DEPT. OF EARTH AND PLANETARY SCIENCES, RUTGERS UNIVERSITY, NJ.

Right: Juliane's water experiment: she melted ice and snow inside the tent, boiled it, carried it outside in a thermos cup and hurled it into the air. The hot water turns to steam instantaneously. CREDIT: JULIANE GROS, DEPT. OF EARTH AND PLANETARY SCIENCES, RUTGERS UNIVERSITY, NJ.

twenty minutes to get dressed into all their layers. They melted ice and snow for the day's drinking water, had breakfast, made a packed lunch, put on more layers and headed off on skidoos to search for meteorites.

At Christmas they opened presents, played Christmas music and enjoyed a special dinner followed by vanilla ice-cream made with lots of snow. New Year's Eve was celebrated with pizza, nachos and snow cones and they greeted the New Year at midnight in full sunshine. Blizzards and windstorms sometimes kept them trapped inside their tents but those were their only days off. They found 263 meteorites in total, from marble-sized to as big as a rugby ball.

I for one will never forget the beautiful bell-like sounds of the blowing snow, the rainbow-sparkling ice crystals on a really cold day, the vast expanses of ice sheets looking like oceans frozen in eternity, the force and strength of the howling winds ripping on our clothes, the funny shaped, icy snotcicles hanging off our frozen noses and beards that made us laugh and turned us into ice monsters, and the icy bite of the wind on any unprotected skin that made us feel so alive and reminded us how vulnerable and precious life really is … And I will NEVER EVER forget the thrill and utter joy of finding a meteorite that you know no one on this planet has ever seen before you. (Juliane Gross, 2 February 2018, ANSMET 2017/2018 field season caslabs. case.edu/ansmet/2018/02/01/goodbye-part-1/)

CHAPTER FIVE

MY JOURNEY

Antarctica New Zealand has sent writers, poets, painters, musicians, photographers, sculptors, dancers, journalists, film-makers and other artists to the ice. In December 2016, I was very lucky to be one of them.

Antarctica was astonishing, exhilarating and beautiful, from the first glimpse of floating sea ice and mountain ranges through the plane window. It

was often challenging, too. I even managed to get lost inside Scott Base, which is almost impossible, seeing as it's one long corridor from end to end.

Richie, the leader of our climb up Castle Rock, told us to keep our carabiners fixed at all times because a fall could be fatal. Mark, our driver, explained that

Left: This is me, outside my tent on our Field Training camp! CREDIT: PHILIPPA WERRY.

Below: Cooking dinner in the snow kitchen that we have just dug out on our Field Training programme. CREDIT: PHILIPPA WERRY.

Right: A memorial to Frank Worsley on the Akaroa waterfront. CREDIT: DAVID WERRY.

Below: Shackleton planted an oak tree in Christchurch at what was then the Girls' Training Hostel (90 Ensors Rd). On the same day, he visited the Captain Scott statue and gave a public lecture about the experiences of the *Endurance* men and the Ross Sea Party. CREDIT: DAVID WERRY.

the Hagglund would float if we went through a crack in the ice and we would get out through the roof. The staff at Scott Base are wonderful and take great care of you, but Antarctica itself doesn't take care of anyone. The environment can change from safe to dangerous to life-threatening in minutes.

I never got over the novelty of glancing out the windows late at night and seeing it still light outside. I loved the interesting conversations over meals and morning and afternoon teas in the dining room. (The food is amazing, thanks to the awesome chefs.) I loved feeling a part of the base – they even put us on the washing up rota.

But the outstanding highlight for me was visiting the historic huts. Walking into them is like walking back into history. It's so special to spend time where the early explorers lived and worked, and it makes you realise all over again how amazing their achievements were.

You can read more about my trip to the ice here: kiwikids2antarctica. blogspot.co.nz

Right and below: The house where Frank Worsley was born in Akaroa, Banks Peninsula. CREDIT: DAVID WERRY.

Left: Robert Falcon Scott memorial oak tree in Arun St., Oamaru. When Pennell and Atkinson came ashore in Oamaru to cable the news of the Polar Party's fate, they walked up this street to the home of the harbourmaster. CREDIT: GAVIN MCLEAN, NZHISTORY, MINISTRY FOR CULTURE AND HERITAGE.

Your journey

You can start being an Antarctic explorer right now. There are many places with Antarctic connections: museums and art galleries, ports and shipyards, churches, town halls, houses, trees, gravestones, gardens, memorials and statues. Five 'gateway cities' around the world have a special relationship with Antarctica: Christchurch (New Zealand), Hobart, Tasmania (Australia), Cape Town (South Africa), Punta Arenas (Chile) and Ushuaia (Argentina).

In Wellington, you can see the Byrd memorial on top of Mt Victoria and Mrs Chippy's statue on Harry McNeish's grave in Karori cemetery. One of the tractors from Edmund Hillary's expedition is at Canterbury Museum, along with one of Fuch's Sno-cats, and one is at MOTAT (Museum of Transport and Technology) in Auckland. (The third one is in the Massey Ferguson Technology Centre in Beauvais, France.) The Sir Edmund Hillary Alpine Centre, in Aoraki Mount Cook village, houses a replica tractor; Hillary trained at Mt Cook before his Everest and Antarctic expeditions.

Hui Te Rangiora is a revered ancestor for the people of Te Awhina marae in Motueka. The tekoteko (carved figure) on the top of their whare tūpuna (meeting house), Tūrangapeke, shows Hui Te Rangiora, gazing out in a quest for new lands. He also sits above the carved waharoa (gateway) at the entrance to Te Puna o Riuwaka in Kahurangi National Park. It is said that he rested here

Above: The Lyttelton graving dock (or dry dock) was built by 300 men over two years and opened in 1883. It could be flooded to let ships enter and then drained so they could be repaired. Scott's ships *Discovery* and *Terra Nova* both used the graving dock, and it is still in use today. CREDIT: DAVID WERRY.

in preparation for his epic trip south. The waharoa is a public space, but to visit the marae you need to follow marae protocol, although you can see the tekoteko from the road.

St Stephen's Church in Peel Forest, Canterbury, has a stained-glass window commemorating Jim Dennistoun, a farmer and mountaineer who sailed on the *Terra Nova*. In World War One, he signed up for the Royal Flying Corps. His plane caught fire and came down behind enemy lines, and he died in August 1916 while a prisoner of war in a German hospital.

In Christchurch you can visit the International Antarctic Centre and see Antarctic exhibits at the Canterbury Museum, a tree planted by Shackleton, statues of Captain Cook and Captain Scott and the site of the Magnetic observatory in the Botanic Gardens. At Godley Head, near Sumner, is a hut from the *Terra Nova* expedition that was meant to be used for meteorological work, but was not offloaded and returned to New Zealand on the ship. Ferries go to Quail Island in Lyttelton Harbour, where dogs and ponies for the early expeditions were kept in quarantine and trained. Lyttelton has the sled dog statue, St Saviour's Chapel, the tug *Lyttelton*, which towed the *Nimrod* out to the harbour entrance, and the graving dock. Frank Worsley's birth place is in Akaroa, and there is a sculpture of him on the waterfront and a display about him in the Akaroa Museum.

In Tasmania, Hobart has museums, a visitor centre at the Australian Antarctic Division, and sculptures of Antarctic explorers (including Amundsen) and animals on the waterfront. Mawson's Huts Replica Museum is a full-scale model of the hut and workshop built at Cape Denison in 1911.

You might see a visiting penguin, leopard or Weddell seal, or a migrating whale heading to warmer waters. You might step outside on a winter's day into a southerly that feels like it's come 'straight from Antarctica'. And who knows – one day, you might be lucky enough to get there!

THE SHIPS

The *James Caird* was brought back to England as cargo on another ship in 1919. It was put on display at Middlesex Hospital to help raise money for the hospital appeal, then given to a friend of Shackleton's, who later gifted it to their old school, Dulwich College in south London, where it is still kept. In World War Two, it survived a bomb blast from a German V1 flying bomb that landed in the school grounds. There are replicas of James Cook's *Endeavour* in Sydney and in Whitby, England, where the original ship was built. Amundsen's *Fram* is on display in Oslo, Norway; the *Discovery* is at Dundee, Scotland and *Ice Bird* is at The Powerhouse Museum in Sydney.

HERE ARE SOME OTHER UNUSUAL ANTARCTIC MEMORIALS

- The bell of the *Terra Nova* is in the stairwell of the Scott Polar Research Institute in Cambridge, England. The bell is rung twice a day, at 10.30am and 4pm, as an invitation for people to meet up for morning coffee and afternoon tea.
- Igloo's grave is at Pine Ridge Cemetery for Small Animals, Boston, under an iceberg-shaped grave stone with the inscription: 'IGLOO. He was more than a friend.' There is a statue of Byrd and Igloo in Byrd's home town of Winchester, Virginia.
- At Hadley's Orient Hotel, Hobart, you can book the Amundsen Suite (the same hotel, but not the same room where Amundsen stayed).
- The South Pole Inn in Annascaul, Co Kerry, Ireland, was opened in 1927 by Tom Crean, who went to the Antarctic three times with Scott and Shackleton and served in World War One.

Shackleton never made it to the South Pole, but Shackleton Crater at the South Pole of the moon is named after him.

To celebrate their work and achievements, three science labs at Scott Base are now named after Pamela Young, Margaret Bradshaw (the first New Zealand woman to lead a deep field science party) and Thelma Rodgers (the first New Zealand woman to winter over).

The writer Roald Dahl, born in Wales to Norwegian parents, was named after Roald Amundsen.

If you feel blue, get on your skiddoo
And swiffle your way through the snow,
Skiddare to be bold even though it is cold
Skiddon't let it lay you low!
Skiddaddle along, singing a song
Skiddoodle what has to be done!
Your heart will skiddance at each fabulous chance
And skididdle-dee-dee at the fun.

Margaret Mahy,
The Riddle of the Frozen Phantom
(Collins, 2001)

Right: Father Christmas at Scott Base riding a Skidoo.
CREDIT: KEVIN RANDLES, 1992–93, ANTARCTICA NEW ZEALAND PICTORIAL COLLECTION.

Sir Edmund was the first person other than a ruling monarch to be featured on a New Zealand bank note while still alive. The Massey Ferguson tractor originally included in the bottom left corner of the same $5 note was later removed to make space for new security features.

Glossary

Antarctic Circle a circle or line of latitude around the earth; the region south of this is the Antarctic

aurora a display of coloured flickering lights that appear in the upper atmosphere

base (in Antarctica) a scientific centre where people live and work

blubber layer of fat below the skin of ocean mammals to help insulate against the cold

cairn a heap of stones (or snow) made as a landmark or memorial

crevasse a deep crack in the ice

depot a place to store food or supplies

frostbite damage to part of the body, caused by exposure to freezing cold temperatures

glacier a huge mass of ice that moves like a slow river

ice breaker a ship especially designed to break a way through the ice

IGY International Geophysical Year (1957–58)

indigenous native to or belonging to a place

magnetic pole where lines of force from earth's magnetic fields come together

migration movement from one area to another, usually at the same season each year

NASA National Aeronautics and Space Administration

NIWA National Institute of Water and Atmospheric Research

plateau a large, fairly flat area of land that is high or raised up above the surrounding land

scurvy a disease that can be fatal; the cause (not known for a long time) is lack of Vitamin C

TIMELINE

1772–1775:	James Cook circumnavigates Antarctica and sails further south than anyone else
27 January 1820	Fabian Gottlieb von Bellingshausen sights the continent of Antarctica
1823	James Weddell discovers the sea now named after him
1841	James Clark Ross in *Erebus* and *Terror* passes through the Ross Sea and discovers Ross Island
1898	Adrien de Gerlache and crew of the *Belgica* are the first to survive an Antarctic winter
1898–1900	Carsten Borchgrevink leads an expedition to Cape Adare
1901–1904	Robert Falcon Scott leads the British National Antarctic Expedition on the *Discovery*
1907–09	Ernest Shackleton leads the British Antarctic Expedition on the *Nimrod*
1910–13	Scott leads the British Antarctic Expedition on the *Terra Nova*
14 December 1911	Roald Amundsen and his team are the first to reach the South Pole
12 November 1912	Bodies of Scott, Edward Wilson and Henry Bowers found in their tent
21 November 1915	Shackleton's *Endurance* is crushed in the ice and sinks
15 April 1916	Shackleton and his crew land at Elephant Island off the Antarctic Peninsula
19–20 May 1916	Shackleton, Tom Crean and Frank Worsley cross South Georgia to Stromness
30 August 1916	Shackleton reaches Elephant Island and rescues the crew left behind
30 July 1923	Ross Dependency (the area administered by New Zealand) established by British Order in Council
1935	Caroline Mikkelsen of Norway lands on Antarctica (probably on an island, not the mainland)
1 July 1957 – 31 December 1958	International Geophysical Year
20 January 1957	Scott Base opens at Pram Point

4 January 1958	Hillary and his team are first to reach the South Pole overland since Scott in 1912
2 March 1958	Sir Vivian Fuchs completes the first overland crossing with the Trans-Antarctic Expedition (TAE)
1 December 1959	12 countries sign the Antarctic Treaty in Washington, D.C., and agree that the continent should be set aside for peace and science
1969–70	Party of six are the first women to reach the South Pole in November 1969
28 November 1979	Air NZ Flight 901 crashes into Mt Erebus, killing 257 on board
1987	New Zealand Antarctic Heritage Trust formed to care for historic sites in the Ross Sea Region
20 January 2007	Scott Base celebrates its 50th anniversary

Useful websites

New Zealand

Antarctic Heritage Trust www.nzaht.org
Antarctica New Zealand www.antarcticanz.govt.nz
The Antarctic Report www.antarcticreport.com
New Zealand Antarctic Society antarcticsociety.org.nz
NZ History nzhistory.govt.nz/politics/antarctica-and-nz

Australia

Australian Antarctic Division www.antarctica.gov.au
Australian National Maritime Museum www.anmm.gov.au/Learn/
    Library-and-Research/Research-Guides/Antarctica-100-Years-Mawson-and-Scott
Mawson's Huts Foundation www.mawsons-huts.org.au

USA

Byrd Polar and Climate Research Center, Ohio State University bpcrc.osu.edu
Field Museum, Chicago www.fieldmuseum.org
United States Antarctic Program www.usap.gov

England

British Antarctic Survey www.bas.ac.uk
British Library: Turning the Pages – Captain Scott's diary www.bl.uk/turning-the-
    pages/?id=12878b6a-36b9-44db-a940-365b21bfe524&type=book
Discovering Antarctica discoveringantarctica.org.uk
Royal Geographical Society www.rgs.org
Scott Polar Research Institute www.spri.cam.ac.uk
UK Antarctic Heritage Trust www.ukaht.org/discover/antarctica-in-the-uk/antarctic-
    collections-in-uk

SOUTH GEORGIA

South Georgia Museum www.sgmuseum.gs/index.php?title=South_Georgia_Museum

JAPAN

National Institute of Polar Research www.nipr.ac.jp/english

NORWAY

The Polar Museum, Tromsø uit.no/om/enhet/artikkel?p_document_id=398471&p_
    dimension_id=88178
Norwegian Polar Institute www.npolar.no/en

OTHER

Cool Antarctica www.coolantarctica.com/Antarctica%20fact%20file/History/
    exploration-history.php
South Pole www.southpolestation.com

CLIMATE CHANGE

NIWA www.niwa.co.nz/education-and-training/schools/students/climate-change-global-
    warming-and-greenhouse-gases
New Zealand Ministry for the Environment www.climatechange.govt.nz
Thin Ice was released on Earth Day 2013. The website thiniceclimate.org has teaching guides
    and resources and lots of extra short videos.

FURTHER READING

Many books have been written about Antarctica, but these are some of my favourites.

To read books and journals by the early explorers, search on sites like archive.org and gutenberg.org for titles like *Through the First Antarctic Night* (Frederick Cook), *The Voyage of the Discovery* and *Scott's Last Expedition* (Robert Falcon Scott), *The Heart of the Antarctic* and *South* (Ernest Shackleton), *Antarctic Adventure* (Raymond Priestley) *Argonauts of the South* (Frank Hurley), *The Worst Journey in the World* (Apsley Cherry-Garrard), *The South Pole* (Roald Amundsen) and *The Home of the Blizzard* (Douglas Mawson).

NON FICTION

Anthony, Jason C. *Hoosh: Roast penguin, scurvy day and other stories of Antarctic cuisine*
    (University of Nebraska Press, c2012)
Darlington, Jennie. *My Antarctic Honeymoon* (Frederick Muller Ltd., 1957)
Griggs, Kim. *On Blue Ice: A not very brave journey to Antarctica* (Random House, 2003)
Harrowfield, David L. *Icy Heritage: The historic sites of the Ross Sea region, Antarctica*
    (Antarctic Heritage Trust, 1995)
Hooper, Meredith. *The Longest Winter: Scott's other heroes* (John Murray, c2010)
Meduna, Veronica. *Science on Ice: Discovering the secrets of Antarctica* (AUP, 2012)
Priestley, Rebecca (ed.) *Dispatches from Continent Seven: An anthology of Antarctic science*
    (Awa Press, 2016)
Tyler-Lewis, Kelly. *The Lost Men: the harrowing story of Shackleton's Ross Sea party*
    (Bloomsbury, 2006)

PICTURE BOOKS AND JUNIOR FICTION

Alexander, Caroline. *Mrs Chippy's Last Expedition* (Harper Collins, c1997)

Grochowicz, Joanna. *Into the White: Scott's Antarctic odyssey* (Allen & Unwin 2017)

Holt, Sharon. *No Survivors: the diary of Jackie Simms, Hamilton 1979* (Scholastic, 2009)

Hooper, Meredith. *Tom Crean's Rabbit: A true story from Scott's last voyage* (Frances Lincoln Children's Books, 2005)

Lawrence, Ian. *The Winter Pony* (Delacorte Press, c2011)

Lester, Alison. *Sophie Scott Goes South* (Penguin, 2012)

McKnight, Diane M. *The Lost Seal* (Moonlight Pub., 2006)

Mahy, Margaret. *The Riddle of the Frozen Phantom* (Collins, 2001)

Marriott, Janice. *Thor's Tale: Endurance and adventure in the Southern Ocean* (Harper Collins, 2006)

JUNIOR NON FICTION

Andrew, Margaret. *Antarctica: The unfolding story* (Waiatarua Publishing, 2004)

Bledsoe, Lucy Jane. *How to Survive in Antarctica* (Holiday House, c2006)

Gouldthorpe, Peter. *No Return: Captain Scott's race to the Pole* (Lothian, 2011)

Grill, William. *Shackleton's Journey* (Flying Eye Books, 2014)

Stenson, Marcia. *Illustrated History of Antarctica* (Random House, 2007)

MAGAZINES

New Zealand Geographic, Australian Geographic and the New Zealand Antarctic Society Bulletin *Antarctic* have articles online.

RADIO, MOVIES AND VIDEOS

Two classic movies are *The Great White Silence*, made by Ponting in 1924, and the 1948 movie *Scott of the Antarctic*. National Geographic's *Survival! The Shackleton Story* includes original photographs and film footage. *La Marche de l'Empereur / The March of the Penguins* is a nature documentary filmed at the Pointe Géologie colony, near the French scientific base of Dumont d'Urville.

The Radio New Zealand and NZ On Screen websites have many programmes, interviews, films and documentaries about Antarctica.

There are many images and videos on the Antarctica New Zealand website, including Anthony Powell's *Frozen South* videos which give a guided tour of Scott Base and show the movement of the sun over 24 hours and the sea ice breaking out at the end of summer.

Google Earth has walkthroughs of McMurdo Station (goo.gl/maps/oG9HC) and Scott's and Shackleton's Huts (artsandculture.google.com/entity/%2Fm%2F09txk5?hl=en-GB)

INDEX